A FIGHTER PILOT'S GUIDE TO

SPIRITUAL WARFARE

A FIGHTER PILOT'S GUIDE TO

SPIRITUAL WARFARE

KEN MARCH

A Division of WINEPRESS PUBLISHING

Pleasant Word (a division of WinePress Publishing, PO Box 428, Enumclaw, WA 98022) functions only as book publisher. As such, the ultimate design, content, editorial accuracy, and views expressed or implied in this work are those of the author.

ISBN 13: 978-1-4141-1094-3
ISBN 10: 1-4141-1094-4
Library of Congress Catalog Card Number: 2007906924

TABLE OF CONTENTS

Introduction

RECENTLY, I HAD the privilege of visiting the Korean War Memorial in Washington, DC. As I walked through the battlefield scene and looked into the faces of the sculpted soldiers, I could not help but identify with their anguished expressions, as they reminded me of similar feelings I had during my combat experiences in the Gulf War. On the wall of the Memorial, the words "Freedom is not free" echoed loud and clear in my heart.

Visiting other monuments and memorials around Washington, D.C., led me to realize that a tremendous price has been paid for our freedoms. Millions of young men and women have served this country, some making the ultimate sacrifice, to provide the benefits of freedom for each of us. As I have sought the Lord on what we are to learn from this experience, He has led me into some tremendous revelations about how the freedoms we have in this country have been attained and maintained. I have seen how the events that transpired in this country's pursuit for freedom closely parallel the spiritual journey we begin when we accept Jesus as our Lord and Savior.

America declared her freedom when the Declaration of Independence was signed in 1776. The Declaration proclaimed—and still proclaims—that everyone in this country has been created equal and has the inalienable right to live free. However, just because we declared ourselves free did not make us free. It took seven years after the Declaration was signed before we realized our freedom by winning the war against Great Britain. Through our victory on the battlefield we became a free nation, but our battle for freedom did not stop at that point. The history of our country is a continuing saga of men and women of all races and all religions, standing up for truth and liberty.

What is it about freedom that made the minutemen unite against insurmountable odds to battle against the British army (the best in the world) at Concord and Lexington? Is freedom worth the price that many men paid in the foxholes in France during World War I? How is the love of freedom so great that during World War II a commander of an army unit who was surrounded at Bastogne during the Battle of the Bulge could defiantly reply, "Aw nuts," when asked to surrender? Is our freedom so precious that its preservation would make men run up a hill on an island they had never heard of, in the face of machine gun fire, to defeat an enemy who would challenge it?

Our country's history is stained in blood from the lives of men and women of all nationalities who believed in the principles of freedom. This country's heritage of sacrifice cannot be forgotten. If we forget the sacrifice that our forefathers made to gain our freedom and allow this country's freedom to be taken from us, those brave men and women who were willing to pay the ultimate sacrifice died in vain.

"Therefore if the Son makes you free, you shall be free indeed" (John 8:36). "And you shall know the truth, and the truth shall make you free" (John 8:32). Just as this country's freedom was costly, our spiritual freedom came at an extraordinary cost. It was through the sacrifice of Jesus, God's only begotten Son, that the benefits of spiritual freedom were won. Isaiah 53:4-5 describes the sacrifice Jesus made and the freedoms purchased for us: "Surely He has borne our griefs and carried our sorrows; yet we esteemed Him stricken, smitten by God, and afflicted. But He was wounded for our transgressions; He was bruised for our iniquities; the chastisement for our peace was upon Him, and by His stripes we are healed." Jesus carried our grief and our sorrows. The wounds He endured made it possible for us to be set free from every wrong (past, present and future) that we have committed. Every bruise He accepted paid for our wickedness; every beating He suffered purchased our peace; every stripe He bore on His back bought our physical healing.

When we receive our salvation, we accept the freedoms that Jesus obtained for us and are declared free. However, the battle for our spiritual freedom never stops. Spiritual warfare comes into play because even though we have been declared free, we must fight to realize and maintain our freedoms in this natural realm. Hebrews 2:14-15 says, "Inasmuch then as the children have partaken of flesh and blood, He (Jesus) Himself likewise shared in the same, that through death He might destroy him who had the power of death, that is, the devil, and release those who through the fear of death were all their lifetime subject to bondage." We have an adversary who wants us in bondage to him, which is why we must learn how to fight to win. If we allow ourselves to be held in bondage to past wrongs, wickedness, fear or ill health, the sacrifices that Jesus endured to win those things for us were suffered in vain.

I spent fourteen out of the fifteen years I served in the United States Air Force as an F-16 pilot. During my tenure, I had the privilege of learning from some of the best combat aviators in the business. I was taught precisely what makes a successful warrior, and I used those lessons in day-to-day training missions as well as in fifty actual combat missions in Operation Desert Storm. Of all the lessons I learned, the one that benefited me the most was the realization that it is impossible to be a great fighter pilot without going through a rigorous training process and then exercising that training on a regular basis.

This truth, and numerous others from the fighter world, directly parallels our spiritual warfare. The Bible often addresses the reality of our engagement in spiritual battles. First Peter 2:11 says, "Beloved, I beg you as sojourners and pilgrims, abstain from fleshly lusts which war against the soul." Ephesians 6:12-13 says, "For we do not wrestle against flesh and blood, but against principalities, against powers, against the rulers of the darkness of this age, against spiritual hosts of wickedness in the heavenly places. Therefore take up the whole armor of God, that you may be able to withstand in the evil day." First Timothy 6:12 tells us to "fight the good fight of faith, lay hold on eternal life, to which you were also called and have confessed the good confession in the presence of many witnesses."

On this earth, there are two kingdoms in operation; the kingdom of God and the kingdom of this world. Colossians 1:13 tells us that when we accept Jesus as our Lord and Savior, "He has conveyed us into the kingdom of the Son." Galatians 5:17 tells us, "For the flesh lusts against the Spirit, and the Spirit against the flesh; and these are contrary to one another, so that you do not do the things that you wish." These scriptures verify that the kingdoms of this world are constantly at war with the kingdom of God's Son. As a result of the conflict between the flesh and the Spirit, we, as Christians, are either engaged in a battle, preparing for battles that will surely come our way, supporting others in spiritual battles, or having a time of rest from a battle.

Most Christians are either unaware of the reality of spiritual warfare or have chosen to ignore it. Evidence of this fact can be seen in the lack of effort that most display in training themselves for battle. After all, if you knew that tomorrow you would be thrust into an actual battle situation, you would probably not spend your last night in front of a television set—at least not until there was certainty that all possible preparations had been accomplished. Many Christians enter their battles ill-prepared and then wonder why they are defeated.

The time has come for Christians to wake up. Ephesians 1:19-20 says, "What is the exceeding greatness of His power toward us who believe, according to the working of His mighty power which He worked in Christ when He raised Him from the dead and seated Him at His right hand in the heavenly places." The great power that God has supplied is only available to those who believe. When we proclaim Jesus as Lord, we are automatically equipped with the most effective weapons in the universe. However, if we fail to recognize and use the weapons we have at our disposal, or fail to believe they will work, we will still be defeated.

In this book, I am not stating that the problems we face are a result of the vast numbers of demons that lay behind every rock. To be honest, most of the problems we face as Christians are not a result of attacks by spiritual forces but are the result of decisions we make to walk according to the flesh and thus reap the fruit of a corrupt world system (see Gal. 6:8). Direct spiritual attacks do occur, but most occur only when we begin to threaten Satan's domain. Unfortunately, if we look around and judge the fruit of many Christians, we will soon come to the conclusion that Satan does not need to waste his forces on most of us. We do a good job of destroying ourselves without his help. This has to change!

I have felt inspired by the Holy Spirit, and I know that what He has helped me write will surely benefit you in your walk with the Lord. I am claiming Isaiah 55:11 for everyone who reads this book: "So shall My word be that goes forth from My mouth; it shall not return to Me void, but it shall accomplish what I please, and it shall prosper in the thing for which I sent it." I would never proclaim to know everything about this subject, but I do know the One who does know it all. I trust this book will open your eyes to the realization that your walk with God requires daily training missions with the certainty of an occasional call to combat duty.

CHAPTER 1

THE RECRUITMENT PROCESS

"AN ARMY OF one," "Accelerate your life" and "Cross into the blue" are all slogans or catch phrases the United States' military uses to entice young men and women to become part of its team. Since evolving into a voluntary force, the military has been forced to rely on catchy phrases and fancy advertising to solicit the participation needed to field a formidable fighting force. In addition, the government allocates a sizeable portion of the defense budget to making the military an attractive place for people to begin a career. Promises are made to these men and women to make them "more than they could be" by providing training for skills they could not afford to receive elsewhere. Large amounts of money are pledged for their college education, and new recruits are given full medical benefits and a guaranteed retirement plan if they stay in the service the required time. The government is required to purchase the commodity of manpower because it knows that without the resources of these talented and trained personnel, our military and the capability to defend our freedom would cease to exist.

During my last two years on active duty, I was one of two narrators for the Air Force's West Coast F-16 Air Demonstration Team. This team is a complement to the Thunderbirds, which is the Air Force's premiere demonstration team. The F-16 demonstration teams perform basically the same function as the Thunderbirds, but they are smaller and less expensive to operate, which enables the military to benefit from more public exposure without the cost of fielding several teams like the Thunderbirds. When I was involved in the demonstration team, there were West Coast and East Coast demonstration teams for both the F-16 and the F-15 aircraft. In addition to the Air Force's teams, the Navy had

1

several F-14 and F-18 demonstration teams, and there was also a Marines AV-8B Harrier team.

Each weekend between April and September, the military invests a lot of money into these events for one main purpose: to make itself attractive to young men and women so that they will consider a career in the military. Additionally, these demonstration teams show the public the capabilities of the military equipment they are buying with their tax dollars and help keep people's perceptions of the military positive.

Just as the military uses catch phrases, the Church uses truthful statements such as "God has a wonderful plan for your life," "you'll never experience true peace until you follow Jesus," and "Jesus loves you and desires that you be saved" to enlist us to become part of God's spiritual team. God loves us and wants us to be on His team so that He can have the ability to fellowship with us. Additionally, He needs men and women to enlist in His formidable fighting force and go into this world system to win the battles He needs won.

Just like the military, God has promised us benefits when we agree to accept the invitation to join His family. Yet the blessings He has promised are far more valuable than any type of compensation a job can offer. God has promised to meet our every need (see Phil. 4:19). He grants us full medical benefits through the stripes laid on Jesus' back (see 1 Pet. 2:24). His retirement plan is beyond what anyone can imagine (see Rev. 21:1).

What does God spend to get us on board? Whatever it takes! John 3:14-18 says, "And as Moses lifted up the serpent in the wilderness, even so must the Son of Man be lifted up, that whoever believes in Him should not perish but have eternal life. For God so loved the world that He gave His only begotten Son, that whoever believes in Him should not perish but have everlasting life. For God did not send His Son into the world to condemn the world, but that the world through Him might be saved. He who believes in Him is not condemned; but he who does not believe is condemned already, because he has not believed in the name of the only begotten Son of God." God allowed the blood of His own Son, Jesus, to be shed in order to show us how much He wants each of us to become part of His team.

In Matthew 18:10-14, we see another example of how much God desires for all people to be saved. "Take heed that you do not despise one of these little ones, for I say to you that in heaven their angels always see the face of My Father who is in heaven. For the Son of Man has come to save that which was lost. What do you think? If a man has a hundred sheep, and one of them goes astray, does he not leave the ninety-nine and go to the mountains to seek the one that is straying? And if he should find it, assuredly, I say to you, he rejoices more over that sheep than over the ninety-nine that did not go astray. Even so it is not the will of your Father who is in heaven that one of these little ones should perish." God will do anything He can to rescue a person from this wicked world system. God loves each one of us more than we could ever imagine.

Now, understanding the loving character of God, we have to assume that if He did not need us here on earth, He would rapture us the moment we were saved so that we could be with Him and not have to endure the trials and tribulations of this world. However, since that does not happen when we are saved, we have to conclude that it is not His plan. The reason God needs us here on earth is because He must work through humans to have an avenue into this world system.

When God created man, He created him to have dominion over everything in this world. When Adam sinned, he gave that dominion over to Satan, making him the god of this age (see 2 Cor. 4:4). Because humans committed high treason and handed this world system to Satan, the only way God can work on behalf of mankind in Satan's domain is through people who have committed their lives to Him and allow Him to work through them. God cannot do whatever He wants in this world system, because this would violate His Word (this will be explained in detail in a later chapter). This is why we, as Christians, must do our part. God did His part by loving us enough to call us out of Satan's domain. Now it is our responsibility to listen to God and discover how we can allow Him to work through us to call others out of this world's darkness.

The military is very particular in its selection of those it allows to serve in its forces, especially in its pilot positions. When I was enduring the Air Force's pilot recruiting process, I was exposed to hours of testing, a thorough physical examination, and psychological evaluations. This process ensures that the Air Force will get the most qualified individuals that are available.

It is a blessing to know that God's selection of warriors works in a considerably different manner from that of the United States' military. God wants everybody to be in His army. First Timothy 2:4 states, "[God] desires all men to be saved and to come to the knowledge of the truth." This is reemphasized by the apostle Peter when he writes in 2 Peter 3:9, "The Lord is not slack concerning His promise, as some count slackness, but is longsuffering toward us, not willing that any should perish but that all should come to repentance."

The Bible is filled with examples of how God chose individuals who were weak, deprived, or cast aside by the world to do His will. Just look at Hebrews 11, which is God's "hall of faith." Noah was thought to be a lunatic, Moses couldn't speak well, Rahab was a harlot, and David was an adulterer. Yet God took these people just the way they were. To be involved in God's army doesn't necessarily require that we are perfect, strong, smart, beautiful, or even that we have a charismatic personality. God merely wants us to make ourselves available to Him. He will become our strength in weakness, He will be our source of wisdom, and He will provide us with every spiritual blessing in the heavenly places (see Eph. 1:3).

Look at Psalm 18: 31-34, which states, "For who is God, except the LORD? And who is a rock except our God? It is God who arms me with strength, and makes my way perfect. He makes my feet like the feet of deer, and sets me on high places. He teaches my hands to make war, so that my arms can bend a bow of bronze." Psalm 19:7 states, "The testament of the Lord is sure, making wise the simple." In Psalm 119:98-100, we are shown beautiful pictures of what studying and meditating on God's Word will do: "You [God], through Your commandments, make me wiser than my enemies; for they are ever with me. I have more understanding than all my teachers, for your testimonies are my meditation. I understand more than the ancients, because I keep Your precepts."

God put men and women on this earth to rule and reign. However, as a result of Adam's sin, God had to institute a plan for man's redemption. Our adversary, the devil, does not want the redemptive plan to happen, which means that our battle with his forces will involve spiritual warfare: "For we do not wrestle against flesh and blood, but against principalities, against powers, against the rulers of the darkness of this age, against spiritual hosts of wickedness in the heavenly places" (Eph. 6:12-13).

The main battle was won when God raised Jesus from the dead. However, God cannot win the continuing battles in the world, which is ruled by the devil, without dedicated Christian warriors who realize that Jesus gave them the authority to conquer Satan. Ephesians 2:10 gives us a clear picture of our purpose while on this earth: "For we are His workmanship, created in Christ Jesus for good works, which God prepared beforehand that we should walk in them." God needs Christian warriors who will speak His Word, submit their hands to do what He wills and allow their feet to go where He directs to accomplish the task of presenting the gospel of Jesus Christ to all the nations.

If you have never made the commitment to join God's army by accepting Jesus as Lord in your life, why don't you do so now? All you have to do to become God's child is accept the sacrifice Jesus made for you. By realizing you cannot come to God except through the sacrifice that Jesus Christ made for you (see John 14:6), you can freely accept Jesus' sacrifice for your sins, knowing that it will enable you to be adopted into the family of God.

If you have accepted Jesus as Lord of your life but are not living like the soldier God wants you to be, it is time for you to accept the responsibilities that come with the privileges of salvation. Start the preparations for battle by studying His Word daily and praying for His direction, and then go out and win the battles He has enlisted you to win. Always remember that *failure is not an option* when God is on your side.

CHAPTER 2

Initial Training

ONCE A PERSON is sworn into the military, there is not much time wasted between the time of enlistment and the commencement of basic training. The military understands the uncertainty of peace and wants each recruit trained as quickly as possible to ensure this country always has a properly trained fighting force. The first stop for every new recruit is some form of basic training. The purpose of this basic training is to transform people from thinking of themselves into people who think of the organization.

Basic training is very regimented and highly disciplined. There are demands put on new recruits that might seem ridiculous to outsiders. What does being able to bounce a quarter off a bed or being able to march in perfect step have to do with learning to be a soldier? These training techniques are used to teach new recruits how to obey without thinking about an order that was given. When trainees are told to jump, they are not to ask "Why?" but "How high?" Commanders must have confidence that the soldiers under them will be willing to obey every command without hesitation, which is why recruits are taught to have tremendous discipline. Their lives—and the lives of many other people—could be at stake if soldiers fail to respond immediately to what they are ordered to do.

There are many non-military people who believe this type of training technique takes away an individual's identity. However, they fail to understand that a combat unit has to operate as a well-oiled machine. There are many parts that must work in concert with one another. For a combat unit to work properly, each part must do its duty without thinking, because the slightest hesitation could throw off the timing and doom an operation to failure.

In every training environment, there are trainees who excel and trainees who perform poorly. The ones who excel are those who obey orders completely and commit everything they have to accomplishing the training to the best of their ability. The ones that perform poorly are the ones who will not exert any extra effort and do only as much as is required to get by. In most military training environments, follow-on assignments are based on the performance of recruits during basic training. The better a recruit performs, the better job he or she will get once basic training is completed. Those trainees who barely get by in basic training will get the undesirable jobs and bases.

As a whole, the Church has not performed well in the "basic training" area. We do a fair job of recruitment, but once people are sworn into the army of God, we do not prepare them for the inevitable spiritual battles that they will encounter. How many times have you heard of people accepting Jesus as their Savior, and then six months later they are nowhere to be found? Most of the time, it is the Church that must take responsibility for failing to train these people adequately.

There are basic principles that each new believer must be taught, and these principles must be taught quickly after the person's salvation in order to equip him or her with the weapons necessary to thwart the inevitable attacks of the enemy. Mark 4:14-20 clarifies this thought:

> The sower sows the word. And these are the ones by the wayside where the word is sown. When they hear, Satan comes immediately and takes away the word that was sown in their hearts. These likewise are the ones sown on stony ground who, when they hear the word, immediately receive it with gladness; and they have no root in themselves, and so endure only for a time. Afterward, when tribulation or persecution arises for the word's sake, immediately they stumble. Now these are the ones sown among thorns; they are the ones who hear the word, and the cares of this world, the deceitfulness of riches, and the desires for other things entering in choke the word, and it becomes unfruitful. But these are the ones sown on good ground, those who hear the word, accept it, and bear fruit: some thirty fold, some sixty, and some a hundred.

The first group hears the Word, but it is stolen before they receive it. The second group receives the Word (they become Christians), but they have no roots (no training) and stumble when the attacks come. The people identified in the third group are Christians, but they allow the things of this world system to distract them from doing what God wants. If Christians are trained properly, they will have a better opportunity to get to the fourth group of people who produce fruit in their lives.

God uses spiritual "basic training" to transform our selfish nature into a nature that loves as He loves. During this time, God may ask us to do seemingly ridiculous things in order to test whether we are willing to follow His commands without regard to how strange they may seem to our human intellect. God needs to see if we ask "Why?" instead of "How high?" when we are told to jump. Unfortunately, many Christians refuse to submit themselves to this training and end up not passing the tests that God gives to them. Failure of these tests often prevents Christians from maturing and, as a result, they remain in a state of basic training for a long time—possibly their whole lives.

Every new believer must be taught the basics: reading God's Word, spending time in prayer, and fellowshipping with other believers. Sometimes new believers will have difficulty understanding why they must read the Bible, pray to a God they cannot see, or make people of faith their primary associates. However, in the same way that the military changes a person during basic training, Christian basic training changes the person from what he or she once was into someone whom God can use.

In Romans 12: 1-2, Paul says, "I beseech you therefore, brethren, by the mercies of God, that you present your bodies a living sacrifice, holy, acceptable to God, which is your reasonable service. And do not be conformed to this world, but be transformed by the renewing of your mind, that you may prove what is that good and acceptable and perfect will of God." We are to lay down our lives and let God change how we think. It is vital for every Christian to realize that training never stops. However, there is a difference between basic training and the continuous instruction we all go through.

As Christians, each of us must evaluate ourselves to determine the type of trainees that we truly are. Are we being diligent in preparing ourselves for the spiritual battles we will face? Have we committed everything we have to the leadership of our Commander and Chief? Are we doing just enough to get by? When He tells us to jump, do we ask "Why?" or do we ask "How high?" When we see Jesus face to face, will He say to us, "Welcome *good* and *faithful* servant?" If we cannot proudly answer any of these questions, we need to begin the process of committing ourselves to becoming the best trainees God has ever seen.

When I committed to joining the Air Force, I had a guaranteed pilot training slot. However, before I was able to go through pilot training, I had to go through Officer Training School (OTS), which lasted three months. It was during this time that I learned how to be a leader in the United States Air Force. During this time, I experienced firsthand what I thought were ridiculous training methods. Others who had been through OTS had relayed to me the things I would have to do while I was a cadet. I knew that folding my underwear a certain way or ensuring there were not any strings (or "cables," as they affectionately called them) hanging from my clothes would not make me a better pilot, but I realized that they would give me a better understanding of how an organization operates. I knew I had to endure the process of basic training in order to establish myself where I really wanted to be—the Air Force's flying program.

I had never really flown to any extent prior to my Air Force experience. My dad was an Air Force pilot, but I only had a few opportunities to fly with him in small rented private planes. By the time I was old enough to fly, my dad had moved into an administrative position, which didn't allow him much time to teach me how to become a pilot.

As I entered the initial phase of my flight instruction, I had an apprehensive excitement. Little time was wasted during the entire pilot training process. On the first day of training, the commander welcomed me and the thirty other young men (there weren't any women in my class) to the place where our dreams could be fulfilled. Soon after all the administrative matters were completed, our instructors came in and handed us a load of manuals, pamphlets, and books and told us, in no uncertain terms, to get to know our aircraft inside and out.

The next few days were spent listening, reading, and studying. We were taught lessons on the physics of flight, which included Bernelli's principals of lift, as well as lessons explaining the effects of different kinds of drag. Other instruction defined various aircraft systems and how the pilot interfaces with each one. It felt as if a fire hose of information had been shot at us. Yet the instructors knew that this information would lay a foundation that had to be set down before any meaningful progression to more difficult tasks could be accomplished. They knew that detailed understanding of the basics would give us something to fall back on when more advanced lessons did not seem to make sense. Personally, I did not want to study all that *stuff*—I just wanted to get in the airplane and *fly, fly, fly!*

Picture 1 T-41

My initial instruction was in the T-41 (see picture 1), which is the Air Force's designation for a Cessna 172. It is a single-engine, propeller-driven, four-seat aircraft. It took off at 60 mph, and its top speed was around 140 mph. We were given nine rides with an instructor and then, if the instructor believed we were ready, we were allowed to fly the aircraft "solo."

When I got into the airplane for my first solo ride, it felt as if my heart was going to explode. I could hardly contain my excitement as I taxied out to the runway for the first time. There wasn't anyone to take the controls if I messed up. The last words of my instructor were, "Remember what you've learned, and you'll do fine." The flight did go well. I had a blast! My dream of being a pilot was finally becoming a reality. But with all the fun I was having flying solo in the T-41, I knew that I still had a lot of work to accomplish before I could become a qualified Air Force pilot.

We were allowed one month to complete the T-41 training. When it was over, I went into the second phase, which was the T-37 flight program.

The T-37 (see picture 2) is a twin-engine jet aircraft that has side-by-side seating. This seating arrangement allows the instructor to be by the student's side to assist if necessary. This seating structure has a calming effect on the student, because he or she can see the instructor right by his or her side. The T-37 took off and landed at around 90 mph and had a top speed of 450 mph.

Picture 2 T-37

It took six months to complete ninety flights, which included aerobatics, formation and instrument flying as well as lots of classroom work. Throughout the T-37 portion of flight training, there were academic tests as well as flight evaluation rides to rate the student's progress. The T-37 training was followed by six months of training in the more sophisticated T-38 "Talon" (see picture 3).

Picture 3 T-38

The T-38 is a twin-engine jet that has tandem seating, which means that the instructor sits behind the student in a separate cockpit compartment. The instructor is there to assist but the student cannot readily see him, which gives the student a sense of being alone. The T-38 took off and landed at around 140 mph and had a top speed of over 1,000 mph.

There were more evaluations during this phase of flight training, after which time I was finally proclaimed to be a qualified Air Force pilot. The completion of the training process was symbolized by pinning a small set of wings on my uniform, signifying to all that I was a *pilot*. The night I received my wings was a time for me to reflect on the tremendous accomplishment of making it through a very demanding training program. Having the ability to be called an Air Force pilot gave me a lot of personal pride.

I related the story of my progression through basic flight training to emphasize the fact that I had to be *trained* to fly advanced aircraft. It took a year of twelve- to sixteen-hour days for me to get into a position where I could graduate from pilot training. Had I jumped into a T-38 on day one and tried to fly, I would have probably killed myself along with anyone else who got in the aircraft's path. It is also important to realize that training aircraft like the T-37 and T-38 cannot accomplish the Air Force's mission. Pilots have to go on to the next level and get qualified in fighters, bombers, tankers and transports to accomplish the mission of defending the United States of America both domestically and abroad.

There are remarkable parallels between the Air Force's pilot training program and the spiritual training that every Christian must go through. Everything we accomplish for God is done through faith, and we can never expect to jump right into the deeper things of God without first learning the basics of faith. If our desire is to do great things for God, we must first master the basic principles of faith so that we can build a foundation of immovable faith. God will instruct us through His Word, through others, and through life situations to get us to the point in which we can do all He has called us to do. This doesn't mean, however, that we are to be totally inactive until we reach that seemingly illusive spiritual point. We are to press forward, knowing that God would never allow us to get into a situation that we were unable to handle.

True spiritual instructors will be gentle and sure as they guide and train us in the deeper things of God. At times, they will sit right beside us so that we know they are there. At other times, we won't be able to see them, but we can be sure that they are right behind us and supporting us with their prayers and words of encouragement. As we progress, there will be times when we mess up—and maybe even completely blow it! Every student makes mistakes from time to time. But that is when the ultimate instructor, the Holy Spirit, will step in and take control of a situation. He is the one who leads us into all truth. As we mature spiritually, He helps us in our weaknesses.

The goal of every instructor is to get a trainee to the point where they do not need him. Spiritual instruction is not any different. There comes a point when the Holy Spirit will require us to stand on our own without having to rely on someone stronger in faith, such as our pastor or a more mature brother or sister in the faith. The trials we go through are lessons to mature us to a level where we can believe God for ourselves.

As we progress in our faith journey, there will be evaluations, or trials, along the way. Before we discuss some of the trials we will go through, it is important to first understand that trials and temptations are very different. We are "tempted" when we are carried away by our own lusts, as explained in James 1:13-16. A "trial," on the other hand, is something that comes from our loving Father in order to push us into a deeper relationship with Him.

One very easy way to tell the difference between a trial and a temptation is to ask ourselves this question: *What would be the outcome if I fail?* If the answer to that question leads to something in our lives being stolen, killed or destroyed, it is not a trial but rather a temptation, which is from the devil. For instance, God would not send in a seducing woman to test the love we have for our wives because if we failed, we might lose our marriage. However, if we lost our job, it might be a trial from God to see if we will trust Him to supply all our needs while we are waiting for a new or better job. Trusting God will not allow us to suffer any loss (outside the realm of persecution). Likewise, a sickness or disease that attacks our bodies is not from God. A loving Father would never put a deadly disease in our body as a trial. God understands that the body is the temple of the Holy Spirit, and He will never do anything to defile or destroy His own temple. First Corinthians 3:16-17 says, "*Do you not know that you are the temple of God and that the Spirit of God dwells in you? If anyone defiles the temple of God, God will destroy him. For the temple of God is holy, which temple you are.*" God would not defile that which is holy.

For too long, we have been blaming God for things that are a result of this corrupt world or things the devil has done. We get into the position of blaming God because we have not been trained to tell the difference between what God does and what happens to us as a result of living in Satan's domain. We must stop smearing the character of our *loving* Father.

James 1:2-4 says, "My brethren, count it all joy when you fall into various trials, knowing that the testing of your faith produces patience. But let patience have its perfect work, that you may be perfect and complete lacking nothing." We are to be joyful about trials. Trials tell us that we have progressed to a point in which God is willing to trust us with a spiritual truth. If we pass the trial, patience is produced. If we fail the trial, our loving Father will continue to instruct us to move us into spiritual maturity. If we fail the test because of laziness or disobedience and fail to repent, we can expect to receive discipline from our loving Father.

One of the best examples of how God operates in the training of His children is demonstrated in the life of David. If you remember, David had a heart for God. Look at how events transpired when he fought against Goliath in 1 Samuel 17. David was sent on a fact-finding mission for his father, Jesse. When David arrived at his destination, he found that "Israel and the Philistine armies had drawn up in battle array, army against army" (v. 21). As David talked to his brothers, Goliath came out and started spouting off with all sorts of taunts. All of the Israelite soldiers were terrified, but David was not afraid because he had a confidence that was built on more than just a casual acquaintance with God. He had an understanding that Goliath was an uncircumcised Philistine who was defying the armies of the *living* God (see v. 26).

When King Saul heard of David, he sent for him. When David told him that he would fight Goliath, Saul replied, "You are not able to go against this Philistine to fight with him; for you are a youth, and he is a man of war from his youth" (v. 33). Read carefully how David replied: "'Your servant used to keep his father's sheep, and when a lion or a bear came and took a lamb out of the flock, I went out after it and struck it, and delivered the lamb from its mouth; and when it arose against me, I caught it by its beard, and struck and killed it. Your servant has killed both lion and bear; and this uncircumcised Philistine will be like one of them, seeing he has defiled the armies of the living God.' Moreover David said, 'The Lord, who delivered me from the paw of the lion and from the paw of the bear, He will deliver me from the hand of this Philistine'" (vv. 34-37).

Can we not sense David's confidence? How did he get faith like that? David used his time tending sheep to train himself. He meditated on God's Word and used small battles to prepare himself to fight the lion and the bear. He then used those lessons to build his faith for the larger battles that would come. Our lives will not be any different. If we want to accomplish great things for God, we have to use the times when nothing significant seems to be happening—as David did when tending sheep—to train ourselves for the times when He will call us into battle.

In today's action-based society, time management has to be a standard for all believers. When receiving our basic training, we cannot afford to waste time. We have to use our time wisely and prepare ourselves for battles that will come. We must be alert to the times when God wants to teach us a basic lesson in spiritual warfare.

Have you taken a personal evaluation to determine where you are in the Christian training process? Would you be ready if God called on you right now to do what seems impossible? Psalms 144:1 says, "Blessed be the Lord my Rock, who trains my hands for war, and my fingers for battle." As Christians, we must submit to the training sessions even though at times they may not make sense. If we continue to pursue the Father, He will show us liberating truths and equip us with power that is not of this world. In the end, if we diligently pursue what God has called us to do and remain faithful, we too will do things that other people can only dream about—and we will watch our spirits soar!

CHAPTER 3

KNOWING YOUR WEAPONS

WHILE FLYING ONE mission in Operation Desert Storm, I was leading a formation of four F-16s against Iraqi Republican Guard tanks. After releasing all of my bombs on the tanks, I decided to strafe (shoot with the aircraft's 20mm Gatlin gun) another tank that I had not already destroyed. Even though I hit the tank numerous times (the gun shoots 100 rounds per second), I did no significant damage to it because the tank's armor was too thick and strong. The gun, in this case, was simply not the proper weapon to destroy the enemy tank.

This same concept occurs in the spiritual realm. We have many spiritual weapons at our disposal that we can use to attack the devil or defend ourselves from his attacks. However, if we are not trained to use the right weapon at the right time, we will not stop the enemy when he attacks, nor will we be effective when we go after his kingdom. For example, if we use the weapon of prayer and ask God to remove the devil off our backs when we should be using the confession of God's Word, we're doing the same thing as shooting small bullets at a heavily armored tank. Spiritual weapons are being employed, but they're not going to stop the enemy.

Paul tried using prayer against a "thorn" in his flesh. In 2 Corinthians 12:8-9, he wrote, "Concerning this thing I pleaded with the Lord three times that it might depart from me. And He said to me, 'My grace is sufficient for you, for My strength is made perfect in weakness.' Therefore most gladly I will rather boast in my infirmities, that the power of Christ may rest upon me." What Jesus had done for Paul was sufficient. Instead of praying about it, Paul needed to realize the strength that he had through Jesus by resisting the devil and making him flee (see Jas. 4:7). We must diligently train ourselves to know which weapon is appropriate for use in any given situation.

Weapons are the tools that soldiers use to defeat their enemies. If soldiers have no formidable weapon, they cannot be effective and will likely be relegated to a support position. The way soldiers optimize the effectiveness of the weapons at their disposal will define the degree to which they stand out as warriors. How many times have movies displayed boot-camp scenarios where the tough old drill sergeant tells his men that their rifle is their best friend? They learn all its components and even learn to disassemble and reassemble it blindfolded. Fighter pilots do virtually the same thing with their weaponry. They study their aircraft's capabilities and limitations to determine the very best methods of employment. They spend months in training squadrons, learning the basics of flying. All that time spent in combat squadrons refines the basics the fighter pilots learn into techniques that optimize the effectiveness of each respective aircraft.

The Air Force's basic pilot training program prepares men and women to fly fighters, bombers, tankers, and transports. These weapon systems support a part of the overall mission of protecting and defending the United States and its people. Pilots are assigned to the various weapon systems based on the needs of the military and how they score on various evaluations during pilot training. If pilots are given a fighter aircraft, they are assigned to a combat squadron. It is in this combat squadron that fighter pilots really learn to optimize the employment of their aircraft. I emphasize the word "employment" because there are many pilots who can fly different fighters well, but to employ it efficiently against the enemy, they must completely know and understand how to best use the fighter and the weapons available on it.

When new pilots arrive at their respective units, they become the "newbees" and are given the menial jobs that are required to keep a unit operating. The way a person handles the menial tasks will determine the rate at which he or she will take on more responsibilities.

Once I completed basic pilot training, I considered myself blessed by being awarded the F-16 "Fighting Falcon" (see picture 4) as my weapon system. The F-16 is a single seat (meaning only one pilot), single engine jet fighter that is used in both the air-to-air (airplane against airplane) and air-to-ground (airplane against ground targets) arenas. Because of its agility and awesome weapons system, the F-16 is considered to be one of the best fighters in the world.

Picture 4 F-16 Fighting Falcon

After six months of learning the basics of flying the F-16, I was assigned to my first combat squadron, the 19th Fighter Squadron (nicknamed the "Fighting Gamecocks") at Shaw Air Force Base in South Carolina. When I arrived as the "newbee," I was given the awesome responsibility of ensuring that the planning room had the required maps for planning missions. I also was responsible for maintaining the squadron's snack bar.

When new fighter pilots first arrive at their squadron, they always assume the role of a wingman. For any mission, there are usually two or more aircraft that participate. A two-ship formation, called an element (an Air Force term), is the basic fighting unit. It is made up of a more experienced leader (called the flight lead) in one F-16 and a wingman in another F-16. This arrangement allows the less experienced wingman to learn from and be protected by a more experienced leader.

One of the main requirements for new fighter pilots is to study, study, and then study some more. A lot of information must be assimilated in a fairly short time. Tests are given to see if pilots have a good understanding of the systems of the aircraft and the weapons it carries. Pilots are also required to know the enemy's aircraft and its weapons and capabilities.

In addition, pilots must have an ability to quickly identify all types of enemy aircraft and certain ground equipment.

All this book knowledge is used in daily training missions. These training missions help to put this head knowledge into something that can be seen and felt. Before every training mission, pilots are given an extensive briefing that lays out the objectives for the flight and how the objectives are to be accomplished. After the flight is completed, the pilots meet to debrief, or explain, how each member of the element performed his or her duties and how each pilot could upgrade his or her performance on the next flight. This training routine goes on day after day, because once pilots learn how best to employ their aircraft, they must continually train to hone, refine, and maintain those skills.

A classic example of the need for this continual training in an F-16 can be seen in something pilots refer to as "basic switchology." The F-16 cockpit is set up so a pilot has the throttle (which controls the power of the engine) in his or her left hand and the control stick (which the pilot uses to maneuver the aircraft) in his or her right hand.

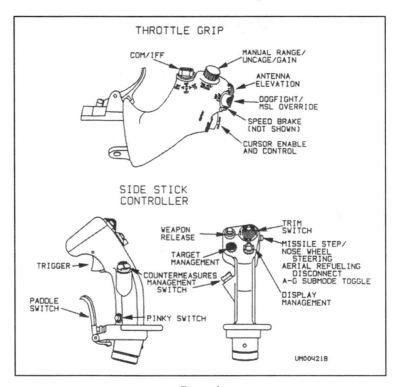

Figure 1

On the throttle, there is a switch to control the two radios, a switch to control where the radar searches, a switch to control the weapon mode, and a missile control button. On the control stick, there is an aircraft trim switch, a radar control switch and a multifunctional display switch (which determines what is shown on the three cockpit video displays). There are also two types of countermeasure switches (these turn the electronic countermeasures on or off and deploy chaff or flares to defeat incoming radar or heat-seeking missiles), the trigger, and a weapons release button. Almost every finger on each of the pilot's hands is used to move one of the various switches. Pilots must study in order to possess the ability to know which switch does what in different positions and practice over and over in order to know how to move the correct switch the required way at the proper time. In the F-16 community, we call this the "advanced piccolo drill," because it is like playing a musical instrument.

The F-16 can be equipped with three different types of weapons to shoot down enemy aircraft (see figure 2). The AMRAAM (Advanced Medium Range Air-to-Air Missile) is a radar-guided missile employed against enemy aircraft that range from two miles away to a range of more than twenty-five miles. The AIM-9M is a heat-seeking missile (one that guides on the infrared energy of an enemy aircraft) that can be employed against aircraft at a minimum of one mile out to a range of about ten miles. Finally, a Gatlin gun can be used against enemy aircraft that are four miles or less from the F-16.

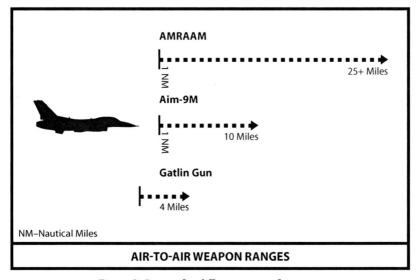

Figure 2: Ranges for different types of weapons

The range of the F-16's weapons overlap so that more than one weapon can be used at different ranges. However, there are some ranges in which only one specific weapon will work. Without each of these three forms of weaponry, a gap will exist where the enemy cannot be effectively engaged.

Christians can learn a lot about how to train themselves spiritually by learning some of the military's techniques. Without spiritual weapons, Christians are relegated to spectator status. They are out of the battle and back cooking meals for the troops. Jesus died and was raised again to give us the authority to be warriors, not cooks!

Second Timothy 2:15 says, "Be diligent to present yourself approved to God, a worker who does not need to be ashamed, rightly dividing the word of truth." Diligence does not convey a casual attitude toward a particular subject. God demands that we be diligent in learning how to use the weapons He has given us. We are to know what weapons we have and how to use them. Just as pilots use different weapons in the F-16 for air-to-air combat, Christians employ different weapons in the spiritual realm. Different weapons will overlap in their effectiveness against the enemy, but there will be times when only one specific weapon will work. Additionally, if we leave out one of the spiritual weapons, there will be holes in our ability to effectively engage the enemy.

Our assignment process into a church family should not be much different from the military's. God has given us specific gifts and talents to use for His glory. We need to pray to receive His assignment to a church where we can use the gifts He has given to us. Ephesians 2:10 tells us, "For we are His workmanship, created in Christ Jesus for good works, which God prepared beforehand that we should walk in them." We need to recognize our spiritual gifts and then allow the leadership of the church where God has assigned us to determine where we would best fit into the family.

Too often, many new (and, unfortunately, some old) Christians will try to do something other than what God has prepared and called them to do. Many times, and for various reasons, people are put in leadership positions before they have the maturity or experience to lead. This normally leads to disaster for the individual and everyone under him or her. Additionally, many new Christians will come into a church and try to take over instead of accepting their role as the "newbee" and being faithful in the position God has for them no matter how menial it may seem.

When we are new believers in Christ, we need to assume the role of a supporting wingman under the leadership of a more mature mentor. By doing this, we can learn from his or her experience while allowing those leaders to keep us out of harm's way. While being mentored, we can use the opportunity to study, study, and then study some more. Then, we need to trust God as He gives us the trials (tests) we need in order to move us on to maturity. James 1:2-5 assures us that He will do this for us: "My brethren, count it all joy when you fall into various trials, knowing that the testing of your faith produces patience. But let patience have its perfect work, that you may be perfect and complete, lacking nothing." Once we are placed in an environment to mature, we must continue to hone our skills in the use of spiritual weapons that we have at our disposal. To explain what I mean, let me share two stories with you.

A while back, I was walking down a street in a bad part of San Francisco. Suddenly, I heard the Holy Spirit say to me, "What would you do if someone came to rob and harm you?" I did not know how to respond. God was using an everyday event to train me for a battle that I might encounter. This is what He told me: "You should say, 'It is unfortunate that the spirit in you [the demon] cannot see the Spirit in me [the Holy Spirit].'" God was revealing who I was in Christ Jesus. He was making the Word, which I had studied, come alive in an everyday situation. Now I use that lesson to constantly prepare myself for just such a situation. If I am ever faced with an attacker, I know what I should do to allow the power of the Holy Spirit to overcome the power of those spirits that would want to harm me.

Another time, I was watching a family as I was eating at a well-known fast-food restaurant. I was probably staring, and the Holy Spirit again began teaching me. He said, "What would you do if the man of the family angrily said to you, 'What are you looking at?'" Again, I did not know what I would say. Once again, God used an everyday event to train me to do battle. He said, "Tell him that you see a family God loves tremendously and one that He wants to see blessed beyond their wildest dreams." I had to sit in awe. I did not get to test it out on that family, but God used the information I knew from His Word and put a practical application to it.

I am constantly amazed at the number of Christians who seem surprised when they are attacked by the devil. Second Corinthians 10:3 says, "For though we walk in the flesh, we do not war according to the flesh." Galatians 5:17 says, "For the flesh lusts [wars] against the Spirit, and the Spirit against the flesh." As long as we are alive on this earth, spiritual warfare will occur in our lives because the Spirit in us is at war with the spirit in the world.

Second Corinthians 10:4-6 continues by saying, "For the weapons of our warfare are not carnal but mighty in God for pulling down strongholds, casting down arguments and every high thing that exalts itself against the knowledge of God, bringing every thought into captivity to the obedience of Christ, and being ready to punish all disobedience when your obedience is fulfilled." Even though spiritual warfare is a fact, we need not fear, because Jesus has already provided the victory for us. Romans 8:37 says, "Yet in all these things we are more than conquerors through Him who loved us." The battles we encounter have already been won through Jesus Christ.

When Jesus died on the cross, He became sin for us and paid the price for our redemption. When He rose from the dead, He defeated Satan and completely gained back the authority that mankind lost when Adam handed over his authority to Satan. Colossians 2:15 reveals how Jesus defeated Satan: "Having disarmed principalities and powers, He made a public spectacle of them, triumphing over them in it." Matthew 28:18 says, "All authority has been given to Me [Jesus] in heaven and on earth. Go therefore [because through Jesus we have that same authority] and make disciples of all nations."

Making disciples of all nations requires us to engage in spiritual warfare because we will have to go into enemy territory to make those disciples. We must therefore have knowledge of the spiritual weapons available to us and possess the ability to effectively use those weapons in order to move the victories we have in Christ Jesus from the spiritual realm into the physical realm. Hebrews 5:14 puts it this way: "But solid food belongs to those who are of full age, that is, those who by reason of use have their senses exercised to discern both good and evil." Without exercising our knowledge and ability, we will continually be defeated when the attacks occur.

The time to prepare ourselves is not when we are going through a battle but before we are faced with such a situation. Unfortunately, most Christians as a whole are very deficient in their ability to use the spiritual weapons at their disposal. Hosea 4:6 tells us the outcome of His children in this situation: "My people are destroyed for lack of knowledge. Because you have rejected knowledge, I also will reject you from being priest for Me; because you have forgotten the law of your God, I also will forget your children."

If we are going to defeat our enemy and win the lost for Jesus, this deficiency must be erased. In the next several chapters, we will examine the spiritual weapons that have been placed at our disposal for us to win the spiritual battles we so often encounter. Remember, we are more than conquerors through Christ Jesus. We need to start acting like it!

CHAPTER 4

THE WEAPON OF THE WORD

SINCE THE BIBLE, which is God's Word, is the weapon that reveals who God is and how all other spiritual weapons work, let's look at it first. Second Timothy 3:16 lets us know that men under the inspiration of the Holy Spirit wrote the Bible. *It is God's Word!* His Word is established in heaven (see Ps. 119:89) and stands forever (see Isa. 40:8). The Bible is our access to the very nature and personality of God. It's our foundational tool, our "owner's manual" that we need to live a successful Christian life. The Bible (God's Word) is described as a light to our path (see Ps. 119:105), a revealer of the will of God for our lives (see Rom. 12:1-2), and a tool to measure the intent of our heart (see Heb. 4:12). Meditating on God's word makes us prosperous (see Josh. 1:8), adds long life and peace (see Prov. 3:2), and provides health for our flesh (see Prov. 4:22). The Word is what we use to build our house on the Rock (Jesus), enabling us to withstand the storms of life that come our way. The Bible is also described as a sword (see Eph. 6:17), which is the weapon given to us for inflicting damage on the enemy when he rises up against us.

Even with all the benefits that accrue from using the Bible, many Christians often do not read or meditate on it in the way our loving Father mandates. As a result of neglecting God's Word, a majority of Christians are living defeated lives, and the world is not being evangelized the way God intends. The enemy has been able to "steal, kill, and destroy" (John 10:10) because we, as Christians, have not used God's Word to understand our rights in this world or how we should use the powerful weapons entrusted to us. As a result, the Christian Church has not been able to meet the needs of the Body or the needs of a lost world.

I grew up in a traditional Christian home. My mother and father were (and still are) beautiful Christian people who truly loved God. However, the churches I attended did not emphasize the importance of reading and meditating on God's Word. (Well, they probably did, but I didn't listen very well.) What I understood was that as long as I comprehended the general principles (which the preacher would help us understand, as he was the one who had spent years studying), I would be fine. As a result, I never studied what the Bible actually said with any intensity. I simply accepted someone else's opinion about what it said and meant.

The Bible never commands us to listen to someone else's interpretation of what God says. The Bible tells us to meditate on the Word and hide it in our heart (see Ps. 119:11). It also tells us to "be diligent to present yourself approved to God, a worker who does not need to be ashamed, rightly dividing the word of truth" (2 Tim. 2:15). Many Christians are defeated when faced with life's adverse situations because they fail to study God's Word. This ignorance of what God's Word says leads to their failure to understand the authority they have in this world system. In addition, when they are attacked by the devil, many of his fiery darts strike their target because their shield of faith, which is developed by reading and meditating on the Word (see Rom. 10:17), is too small to protect them. They also lack the expertise to use the Word, which is their sword (see Eph. 6:17), to defend themselves.

Even though most of us realize the need to read and meditate on the Bible, many of us simply do not do it because we believe the Bible is too difficult to understand. What kind of God would give us instructions on the type of life He requires us to live that were too difficult to understand? This belief that God does not want us to completely understand His Word goes completely against the nature of God. He gave His inspired Word so that we could understand how we are to live our lives. The problem is we have "religionized" God's Word to the point of making it incomprehensible. We have been taught that the way to really understand "God's Holy Book" is to get several different commentaries or go to a seminary to study under "experts" who know what it says. Please don't misunderstand me; commentaries are beneficial, and there are valid reasons for men and women to be trained for Christian service. However, a person does not need a seminary degree to understand what the Bible says.

God's Word has to be revealed to us through His Spirit before it can be used to make any significant changes in our lives. Romans 10:17 tells us,

"So then faith comes by hearing, and hearing by the word of God." The Greek word translated as *word* in this passage is *rhema*, which means an utterance. Faith comes when God uses His written Word to speak to our spirits. The only way for God to speak to our spirit is for our spirit to be in communion with Him. The only way for our spirit to be in communion with Him is to have our dead (separated from God) spirit recreated into a spirit that is alive. The only way for our spirit to be recreated is to accept the sacrifice Jesus Christ made for us on the cross. So you can see that the *only* requirement for God's Spirit to speak to our spirit is for us to have a relationship with the Father through Jesus Christ!

Reading the Bible should be an active time between our heavenly Father and us. That is why Hebrews 4:12 says, "The word of God is living and powerful." God directs His Holy Spirit to teach and reveal His Word to us when we desperately desire Him. It is through His Word that He reveals Himself to us. We can see His character, His heart and His desire for our lives. It is an alive and active relationship! As we dedicate ourselves to the study of God's Word, we can then use commentaries or formal training to understand the context of Scripture. However, we must trust the living God to accurately show us what He wants us to see in His Word in order to arm us with the weapons we will need to fight our daily battles.

It is true that there are some things in the Bible that are difficult to understand. However, the primary reason for this is not because God is hiding something from us but because our minds, which have been trained in the ways of the world, cannot comprehend how God does things. For example, grace is one attribute about God that our minds cannot comprehend. Knowledge gained from commentaries or seminaries can teach us the meaning of the word, but only God's Spirit can reveal the vastness of God's grace.

Isaiah 55:8-9 tells us, "'for My thoughts are not your thoughts, nor are your ways My ways', says the LORD. 'For as the heavens are higher than the earth, so are My ways higher than your ways, and My thoughts than your thoughts.'" This scripture is talking about the mystery of grace as it pertains to the forgiveness we receive when we confess our sins to our loving Father. We will never be able to comprehend with our minds the grace we are given through forgiveness. God does not just forgive us; He forgets the sin ever happened. Psalm 103:12-14 says, "As far as the east is from the west, so far has He removed our transgressions from us. As a father pities his children, so the LORD pities those who fear Him. For He knows our frame; He remembers that we are dust."

Jeremiah 31:34 says, "For I will forgive their iniquity, and their sin I will remember no more." What a freeing thought! Through our acceptance of God's grace, we become righteous (have right standing) before the God who created everything around us. Regardless of what we have done, our repentance and acceptance of the sacrifice that His Son, Jesus, made for us enables us to come boldly before His throne as a son would before his own father (see Heb. 4:16). When we do come before Him, God doesn't see anything but Christ Jesus, because we have put on Christ (see Gal. 3:27). These are scriptural facts about grace. However, we are mentally incapable of understanding how God forgives us. Until these facts are revealed to our spirit through His Spirit, we will continually come whimpering to the Father about how low we are and how we are so unworthy of His love. But once we see these scriptures through the Spirit, we have the ability to believe that we are truly forgiven and cleansed (see 1 John 1:9) and can boldly stand righteous before our God.

First Corinthians 2:9 says, "But as it is written: 'Eye has not seen, nor ear heard, nor have entered into the heart of man the things which God has prepared for those who love Him.'" I have always been told that this scripture was referring to heaven. However, when you look at the context of the scripture, you find that heaven is never mentioned. In fact, this scripture is talking about the wisdom of God. Verse ten says, "But God has revealed them to us through His Spirit." Our physical eyes or ears can never see the wonderful things God has in store for us. It is only through our spiritual eyes and ears that we can get the full depth of God's wisdom and the wonderful things He has in store for us.

I first began to understand the importance of God's Word during my freshman year in college. After God revealed to me His power and the importance of His Word, I became passionate about taking the time to intensely read and study the Bible. I read it in the morning, in between classes, and the Bible was the last book I read at night. As I read, I purposed in my heart to believe what it actually said. It did not take long before I discovered that many of my ideas about God had to change, as many of the things I had been taught did not line up with what the Bible actually said. God, through His Word, started the process—a process that never ends—of renewing my mind to think like He thinks.

When I first started reading God's Word, I was led to the first chapter of Ephesians. In this passage, Paul prayed a prayer for the saints in the church in Ephesus and for faithful saints in Christ Jesus (see v. 2). In verses 17-20, he prayed, "That the God of our Lord Jesus Christ, the

Father of glory, may give to you the spirit of wisdom and revelation in the knowledge of Him, the eyes of your understanding being enlightened; that you may know what is the hope of His calling, what are the riches of the glory of His inheritance in the saints, and what is the exceeding greatness of His power toward us who believe, according to the working of His mighty power which He worked in Christ when He raised Him from the dead and seated Him at His right hand in the heavenly places." I believed that I was a faithful saint, so I substituted my name into this scripture. Virtually every time I read the Word, I would pray this prayer:

> I pray that You, God, the God of my Lord Jesus Christ, the Father of glory, may give to me the spirit of wisdom and revelation in the knowledge of You, that the eyes of my understanding may be enlightened, that I may know what is the hope of Your calling, what are the riches of the glory of Your inheritance in the saints, and what is the exceeding greatness of Your power toward me who believes, according to the working of Your mighty power that You worked in Christ when You raised Him from the dead and seated Him at Your right hand in the heavenly places.

First John 5:14-15 says, "Now this is the confidence that we have in Him, that if we ask anything according to His will, He hears us. And if we know that He hears us, whatever we ask, we know that we have the petitions that we have asked of Him." The things we pray from God's Word are His will, and this scripture in 1 John tells us that He will always answer a prayer that is according to His Word because His Word is His will.

As God began to reveal Himself to me in mighty ways, I began to see His love directed toward me. Scriptures began to leap off the page and into my spirit. There was nothing else (and there still is nothing else) that I would rather read. I began to understand there is life in the Word of God! I finally identified with the psalmist when he said, "As the deer pants for the water brooks, so pants my soul for You, O God." The Word became my umbilical cord to God Almighty.

In Psalm 119:105, the Word is described as a lamp and a light. The psalmist used this metaphor to explain that when things don't make sense and all we can see is darkness, the Word will light our way. Psalm 119:130 says, "The entrance of Your words give light." God wants us to know what is involved in His will for our lives.

I originally went to college to study veterinary medicine. However, during my sophomore year in college, God revealed to me that veterinary medicine was not His will for my life. Because I had totally committed myself to Him, I started seeking what He wanted me to do. After a year of praying and searching, I shared with a friend the frustration I was feeling about finding God's will for my life's profession. In response, my friend told me this simple but profound truth: "If God wills us to do something for Him, it is His responsibility to tell us what that something is. It would be unfair for God to expect us to read His mind."

When I realized the depth of that statement, it relieved much of the stress that came with the decision process. God was responsible for communicating with me! He was the One who would open the doors for me! My only responsibility was to listen and be ready to walk through the doors that He opened. God had already prepared the way for me, just as it is stated in Ephesians 2:10: "For we are His workmanship, created in Christ Jesus for good works, which God prepared beforehand that we should walk in them." God was molding me into a vessel that He would use for the purposes He intended. All I had to do was pray, read and follow Him. And as I meditated on His Word, a light began to shine so intensely on the door of becoming an Air Force pilot that I could not help but walk through it.

In Romans 12:1-2, Paul says, "I beseech you therefore, brethren, by the mercies of God, that you present your bodies a living sacrifice, holy, acceptable to God, which is your reasonable service. And do not be conformed to this world, but be transformed by the renewing of your mind, that you may prove what is that good and acceptable and perfect will of God." It is the Word of God that renews our minds so we can think as God thinks. It is our navigational device provided by God to show us where He wants to lead us!

One of the first areas to be renewed in my thinking was the difference between the physical and the spiritual. As we grow up, we are taught to believe what our senses tell us. Our brain receives inputs from what we feel, see, hear, smell, and taste. It then processes those inputs, and we make our decisions based on how we have trained ourselves to react to that information. When we accept Jesus as Lord in our lives, our sense of what is truth must change. The Word of God must now take authority over the things we feel, see, hear, smell or taste because we can trust only what God says about a matter as *truth*. Galatians 2:20 says, "I have been crucified with Christ; it is no longer I who live, but Christ lives in me; and the life which I now live in the flesh I live by faith in the Son of God, who loved me and gave Himself for me."

The life that we live in the flesh has to be lived by *faith*. When our physical senses tell us something that conflicts with what the Word of God says, what God says in His Word must take precedence over what our senses are telling us. Second Corinthians 4:16-18 says, "Therefore we do not lose heart. Even though our outward man is perishing, yet the inward man is being renewed day by day. For our light affliction, which is but for a moment, is working for us a far more exceeding and eternal weight of glory, while we do not look at the things which are seen, but at the things which are not seen. For the things which are seen are temporary, but the things which are not seen are eternal."

As Christians, we now have two sets of information to process: the spiritual and the physical. For example, we have all felt that we were not saved at one time or another during our Christian walk. How do we fight those feelings? We fight them with the Word of God. The Word takes authority over how we feel. We know we are saved because the promises in God's Word tell us we are!

A prime example is the story of the twelve spies Moses sent to investigate the Promised Land. Ten came back with a bad report, but two spies, Caleb and Joshua, came back with a good report. "Then Caleb quieted the people before Moses, and said, 'Let us go up at once and take possession, for we are well able to overcome it'" (Num. 13:30). Joshua and Caleb had seen the same giants as the others had seen, but their confidence was in God. "And they spoke to all the congregation of the children of Israel, saying: 'The land we passed through to spy out is an exceedingly good land. If the LORD delights in us, then He will bring us into this land and give it to us, a land which flows with milk and honey. Only do not rebel against the LORD, nor fear the people of the land, for they are our bread; their protection has departed from them, and the LORD is with us. *Do* not fear them'" (Num. 14:7-9).

God was displeased with the people because of their unbelief. "Then the LORD said to Moses: 'How long will these people reject Me? And how long will they not believe Me, with all the signs which I have performed among them?'" (v. 4 - 11). However, Caleb pleased God: "But My servant Caleb, because he has a different spirit in him and has followed Me fully, I will bring into the land where he went, and his descendants shall inherit it" (v. 24). If any of us have ever stood on a promise of God, we have been forced to ignore the physical and accept what God's Word says about the circumstance. Once we stand on God's Word, our faith brings the promise from the spiritual realm into the physical realm.

As I have ministered to different people about believing God for a promise, I have often heard them say, "But I need something of substance I can hold on to." When we are facing life's tough situations, we do need something of substance to grasp. However, it cannot be what our senses tell us. We must hold on to that which is stated in Hebrews 11:1: "Now faith is the *substance* of things hoped for, the evidence of things not seen" (emphasis added). It is God's Word that produces faith, and that faith is a substance that provides proof for those things that are not seen.

When we have a cold, we want something of substance to relieve our itching eyes, our cough and our runny nose. So we reach for a pill (a thing of substance) that will make us feel better. We take one or more every six to eight hours until our symptoms are relieved. We do this because that is what the directions on the box tell us to do. Why don't we apply those same principles to God's Word? When Satan tempts us to fear, why don't we search the scriptures to build our faith (the substance) and then use those scriptures on Satan until the pest flees? That is what God's Word instructs us to do! Jesus knew the importance of using the Word against the devil. In Luke 4, Jesus' reply to all three of Satan's temptations was, "It is written" or, "It has been said." If Jesus felt it was important to use the Word when He was tempted, I believe we ought to do likewise.

The Word also reveals our heart's true desire. Hebrews 4:12 tells us, "For the word of God is living and powerful, and sharper than any two-edged sword, piercing even to the division of soul and spirit, and of joints and marrow, and is a discerner of the thoughts and intents of the heart." When I was taking a college chemistry course, our class was assigned the task of identifying several different types of compounds. One of the first steps in the identification process was to determine if the substance was acidic or basic. We used a piece of litmus paper to help identify the substance's properties. If the paper turned blue, it was basic; if it turned pink, it was acidic.

In our lives, we are faced with major decisions about what career to pursue, whom to marry, where to live, what church to attend, the proper vehicle to drive, what clothes to wear, and a myriad of other decisions that are too numerous to list. In all of these decisions, we have to identify God's will. If we are to live a life that is pleasing to the Lord, we must use the litmus test of the Word to judge whether we are making decisions with God's help or whether we are basing our decisions on our own selfish desires. As we meditate on God's Word, we can purify our thoughts and intentions to align them with what God wants for us. Psalm 119:11 says, "Your word I have hidden in my heart, that I might not sin against You!" We all desire to walk a life pleasing to the Lord, but if we are going to accomplish that goal, we must spend time in the Word so that God's desires override those of our own.

The final item I want to share is the fact that the Bible is our weapon against the enemy. In Ephesians 6:17, Paul calls the Word of God a "sword." The sword is a very basic weapon, but was one of the most sophisticated weapons of its time. I believe that if the Bible had been written today, the Word would be described as an F-16, as the F-16 is a very powerful weapon (not that I'm partial or anything).

The Word is one of the weapons that God has provided to us so we can fight and win the battles we encounter. The offensive purpose of the sword is to inflict severe harm on the enemy. When used defensively in conjunction with the shield of faith, it is able to deflect swiping blows from the enemy. For example, if we are being tempted by the devil, he is attempting to inflict harm on us by shooting at us with his cunningly devised fiery darts. How should we respond? What did Jesus do when He was tempted? He didn't ask His Father to relieve Him of the attack, because He knew prayer was the wrong weapon to use in that situation. Jesus deflected the temptations by using the Word! God has told us that if we will resist the devil, he will flee from *us* (see Jas. 4:7). He has already provided the victory! When the devil comes after us, we should do what Jesus did and use the Word. The Word is our offensive weapon that will set the enemy to flight. When we use it on the devil, he *has* to flee.

Why is the Word so important? It is important because it is the Word of God that produces faith. Romans 10:17 says, "Faith comes by hearing and hearing by the *word* of God" (emphasis added). Fear and doubt are opposites of faith. Fear is what the devil uses to steal our joy by implanting all sorts of terrible ideas in our minds to create worry and tension. Doubt is a weapon that the devil uses to try to get us into a position in which we do not care to resist him. When we get to that position, we will accept anything he throws our way, because we have been led to believe that we cannot do anything about the situation anyway. The only counter to those attacks is the Word of God. The Word is what produces the "substance of things hoped for, the evidence of things not seen" (Heb. 11:1). Faith is what counteracts the fear and doubt and connects us to the power of God. It is the *power* of our loving Father that can change any situation we may encounter because, as Luke 1:37 says, "with God nothing will be impossible!"

If you have never spent time in God's Word, today is the day to start. I believe it is good to start with the book of John and then move to the Epistles. But don't just read the Bible because you believe reading it is what you should do. Read the Word because you know abundant life cannot be found anywhere else except in God's presence and because the only way to come to God is through His Word. Also, don't read too fast. Allow God to minister and teach you through His Word. Don't let church traditions restrain or bind the message that God is revealing through His Word. When He says you can have abundant life—which He does say in John 10:10—believe it! If Jesus says you will do greater things than He did because He goes to the Father (see John 14:12), believe Him, for His Word is trustworthy. God's Word is a formidable weapon that will enable you to prosper in anything you do!

CHAPTER 5

THE WEAPON OF FAITH

ON MY FIRST mission in Desert Storm, twenty aircraft from my squadron were sent out to destroy several SAM (surface-to-air missile) sites in Kuwait. We studied the plan that had been developed and believed (or had faith) it would work. It would have been foolish for us to go against the enemy without believing our tactics would accomplish the mission we were tasked to perform. Without proper preparation and training, each of us would have turned and headed for home at the first sign of opposition. Even though many of us had never been in an actual combat situation, we had an idea of what to expect and a belief in our tactics, which allowed us to continue when things got rough. Have you built up your faith sufficiently to believe that God's tactics will work in the spiritual battles you are going through or will go through? If you have not, you'll end up quitting the battle at the first sign of adversity and allow the devil to win those battles.

Faith is another one of the major weapons available to the believer. To get an understanding of faith, we first must understand what it is, why God requires it and how to use it. Without knowing these basic principles of faith, we will go through life not understanding why things happen to us and will lack the urgency to develop our faith to the level God desires.

Webster's Dictionary defines faith as an "unquestioning belief" or a "complete trust or confidence." Hebrews 11 provides the biblical starting point for understanding faith. The first verse defines faith: "Now faith is the substance of things hoped for, the evidence of things not seen." As I mentioned in the last chapter, "substance" is defined as the real or essential part of anything. When we pray for something, faith is the

37

substance that brings the answer to that prayer from the spiritual realm into the physical realm. Faith becomes the evidence that brings the answers to our existing prayers even though we can't see the answer with our physical eyes. When Satan begins to throw words of doubt and fear at us, it is faith in God's character that provides the proof to counter those attacks. When we have faith, we *know* (have complete confidence) that God *will* perform those things He has promised in His Word.

Before we can receive anything from God, faith must be involved. We see this very clearly in Matthew 9:27-30: "When Jesus departed from there, two blind men followed Him, crying out and saying, 'Son of David, have mercy on us!' And when He had come into the house, the blind men came to Him. And Jesus said to them, '*Do* you believe that I am able to do this?' They said to Him, 'Yes, Lord.' Then He touched their eyes, saying, 'According to your faith let it be to you.'"

The question that often comes up is why we need faith to receive from God. The Bible tells us that God is love (see 1 John 4:8) and that He has blessed us with every spiritual blessing in the heavenly places (see Eph. 1:3). He sent Jesus to give us abundant life (see John 10:10), and He wants to give us all things freely (see Rom. 8:32). So why do we have to fight the good fight of faith to receive (see 1 Tim. 6:12)?

When we look at the character of God, we realize that there is a reason for every requirement God puts on us. The requirement of faith is not any different. God wants every person blessed in all areas of their lives. But He had to put a hedge around His blessings to prevent His enemies from having access to them. So, He implemented this principal called "faith" and made everyone who comes to Him operate in faith. Hebrews 11:6 says, "But without faith it is impossible to please Him, for he who comes to God must believe that He is, and that He is a rewarder of those who diligently seek Him."

If God did not put a restriction on access to His goodness, anyone could partake of His blessings—even His enemies. The reason this is true is because God loves unconditionally. He does not look on a person's goodness or inadequacies as the basis for determining His level of giving. He has already made the decision to love, so He has also made the decision to give. This can be clearly seen in John 3:16: "For God so loved the world [not his chosen ones, but the very system that required the death of His Son] that He gave [love always has action to it] His only begotten Son." God is a lover and a giver! He had to put a restriction on the ability to receive what He naturally gives.

Faith is that restriction. Anybody who walks in faith can have what God naturally gives. Look at Galatians 5:6: "For in Christ Jesus neither circumcision nor uncircumcision avails anything, but faith working through love." The reason faith becomes the hedge to all the goodness that God has is because it must work through love in order to operate. God's enemies are incapable of walking in love because they are concentrated on self. If we do not have love, we cannot have faith, for faith works through love. If we do not have faith, we cannot receive the goodness of God. It is still there for us, but we cannot receive it.

For this reason, faith is one of the foundational weapons that must be mastered if we are to accomplish anything for the kingdom of God. Jesus said in John 14:12, "Most assuredly, I say to you, he who believes in Me, the works that I do he will do also; and greater works [greater in number] than these he will do, because I go to My Father." Acts 1:8 tells us, "But you shall receive power [the Greek word is *dunamis*, meaning miraculous power] when the Holy Spirit has come upon you; and you shall be witnesses to Me in Jerusalem, and in all Judea and Samaria, and to the end of the earth." Wonderful, miraculous and seemingly unbelievable things can be realized through faith.

Faith can be compared to a nuclear weapon. A nuclear bomb is relatively small. Inside the bomb, a chain reaction is started that builds until it reaches critical mass and creates a massive explosion. Faith starts a chain reaction by connecting our unrighteous selves with our righteous Father, who then directs the Holy Spirit to explode on the scene and exert miraculous power on our behalf. Just like a nuclear device, it doesn't take much faith to move a mountain (see Matt. 17:20-21).

If our aim is to please God, we must come to Him in faith, because it is impossible to please Him without faith (see Heb. 11:6). Hebrews 11:33-40 tells us some of the tremendous accomplishments wrought through faith:

> Who through faith subdued kingdoms, worked righteousness, obtained promises, stopped the mouths of lions, quenched the violence of fire, escaped the edge of the sword, out of weakness were made strong, became valiant in battle, turned to flight the armies of the aliens. Women received their dead raised to life again. Others were tortured, not accepting deliverance, that they might obtain a better resurrection. Still others had trial of mockings and scourgings, yes, and of chains and imprisonment. They were stoned, they were sawn in two, were tempted,

were slain with the sword. They wandered about in sheepskins and goatskins, being destitute, afflicted, tormented—of whom the world was not worthy. They wandered in deserts and mountains, in dens and caves of the earth. And all these, having obtained a good testimony through faith, did not receive the promise, God having provided something better for us, that they should not be made perfect apart from us.

Eighteen of the forty verses in Hebrews 11 start with the words "By faith." This very fact should show us that our accomplishments for God must be done by *faith*.

All of us have some sort of faith, and all of us know how to exercise our faith. If someone offers us a chair to sit in, we immediately look at the chair and evaluate its capability to hold us. We use our ability to determine whether the chair would hold us and then exercise our faith by sitting in the chair. We developed that faith by repeatedly sitting on chairs and not having those chairs collapse on us. In the same way, when we drive down a two-lane road, we exercise our faith in the drivers coming in the opposite direction by not veering away from every car we pass. We can do this because we have passed many cars without having one come into our lane. Everything we do is based on a belief or faith in something. It is a faith that has been developed through what we have seen, heard, touched, smelled, or tasted.

Now let's say a good friend of ours offers us a chair to sit in that looks as if it is ready to fall apart. If we decide to sit in the chair, we do so based on faith in our friend and not in the chair. We let our faith in our friend override our lack of faith in the chair. When my sons were learning to jump into a swimming pool, I would get into the water and encourage them to jump by calmly letting them know I would not allow them to sink. They had never jumped into a pool and had no way to know what would happen if they did. But they knew I loved them and would not want anything bad to happen to them. Once they placed their confidence in the belief that I would not let them sink, they jumped into the pool.

Faith in God is not any different than our faith in sitting in chairs, passing oncoming traffic in cars, or jumping into a pool. When we first start on our faith journey, we do not have a lot of experience to hold us up. We must demonstrate our faith in God by having enough confidence to obey Him when He asks us to jump into areas He has called us even though we may fail to see where they may lead. We can do this because we have confidence that He will be there to catch us and support us. We also show confidence in His character when we believe that He will provide whatever He has promised us in His Word.

Now, before we continue, it is necessary to explain an important aspect of Christian faith. As we encounter various temptations (such as sicknesses or emotional or financial problems) or things related to this corrupt world, there are some that tell us victory will come only after we quote scripture after scripture to develop our faith. The passage people use often use to support this claim is Romans 10:17: "So then faith comes by hearing, and hearing by the word of God." While it is true that quoting passages of the Bible is very beneficial, many Christians have been caught in the trap of thinking that reciting scriptures is some sort of formula that will bring the answer. For instance, it is often said that if we quote the healing scriptures, healing should come to us. Likewise, if we quote the prosperity scriptures, prosperity will come. Don't misunderstand me: I know God's Word is one of the most powerful weapons on this earth. However, just quoting Scripture is not going to produce faith. We must meditate on His Word.

Christian faith is produced when we use God's Word in conjunction with spending time with Him. As we mentioned, the Greek word for *word* used in Romans 10:17 is *rhema,* which refers to the spoken word, rather than *logos,* which refers to the written word. During our times of meditation, the Holy Spirit speaks to us, which then becomes God's spoken word that enables us to develop our confidence in God. When we are sick, it is God's Word that tells us He put stripes on Jesus' back for our healing. It is our meditation on His Word that allows us to see that our loving Father doesn't want us to be sick because we not only read it but we also hear Him say it to us. When we realize the Creator of the universe made provision for us to be well and stay well, we can better put our faith in Him to heal our bodies.

We can quote healing scriptures all day long, but until those words from God instill a trust and confidence in Him, they will not do us any good. Meditation (thinking deeply and praying about something) allows the Holy Spirit to bring to life God's written Word, which our minds then absorb as we read the Word. The written word (*logos*) now becomes the spoken word (*rhema*), which helps us to build a relationship with our Father. This relationship builds our faith to a point that we have the utmost confidence in His ability to perform that which He has said He would do.

To live a faith-filled life, we must know the character of God, acknowledge His wonderful attributes and understand that He desires nothing but the best for us. The following attributes of God reveal His character to us. Once we know and fully understand these characteristics, we can develop an unwavering confidence in our heavenly Father.

- God is love (1 John 4:16-19).
- God is our strength and our shield (Pss. 28:6-9; 84:11; Prov. 30:5).
- God is a protector (Is. 54:9-17).
- God is righteous (Dan. 9:14).
- God is a merciful God (Deut. 4:31; Pss. 100:5; 116:5; 2 Chron. 30:9; Jas. 5:11).
- God is wise in heart and mighty in strength (Job 9:4; 36:5; Ps. 147:3-15).
- God is a just judge (Job 34:17; Ps. 7:11; Isa. 45:21; Rev. 15:3).
- God is a refuge (Deut. 33:27; Pss. 18:1-3; 46:1-11; 62:8).
- God is holy (Josh. 24:19; 1 Sam. 2:2; Ps. 99:9; Isa. 6:3; 1 Pet. 1:16).
- God is gracious, merciful and a giver of perfect gifts (Ps. 103:8-13,17-18; Jas. 1:17-18, 1 Pet. 2:3).
- God's ways are perfect (Ps. 18:30-32).

God desires that we know Him! Knowing God builds our confidence in Him, which in turn builds our faith in what His Word says. In Ephesians 1, Paul prayed that the Ephesians might know God. He emphasized that call again in Philippians 3:10: "That I may know Him and the power of His resurrection, and the fellowship of His sufferings, being conformed to His death."

Religion tells us that we can't figure out what God is going to do. *Yes we can!* If we read His Word, we will see that He is doing what is *best* for *us* according to His plan! In Ephesians 5:17, Paul reinforces this idea by telling us, "Therefore do not be unwise, but understand what the will of the Lord is." Because of this lack of understanding, we often blame God for many of life's difficulties. However, we must have confidence that God desires only the best for us. It is vitally important that we rid ourselves of negative attitudes about God. Only when we see the positive attributes of our *loving* Father can we put our complete faith in Him. Where there is complete faith, there is no room for fear. First John 4:18 says it best:

"There is *no* fear in love; but perfect love [the kind that comes from God] casts out fear, because fear involves torment [God will not torment anyone!]." Only as we come to know that we are loved perfectly will we be able to put the weapon of faith into full operation in our lives.

We must constantly ask ourselves if we have complete faith in our Father. When Paul writes in Ephesians 3:20 that God will do exceedingly and abundantly above all that we could ask or think, do we believe it? When Jesus says in John 10:10 that He came to give us life more abundantly, do we believe Him? When Paul writes in Galatians 3:14 that "all the blessings of Abraham might come to the Gentiles in Christ Jesus [these blessings are found in Deuteronomy 28]," do we choose to walk in those blessings? If not, then is God—who has provided everything—at fault, or are we the ones who fail to believe or put our faith in His Word?

Satan will do anything possible to thwart our confidence in God. The devil knows that if we do not have faith in the character of God, he can defeat us. These attacks on God's character will come through deception, temptation, circumstance, people, and religion. We must realize that God is not a father who breaks our arm just to get our attention or allows someone to die just to save someone else. God is good at all times and in every situation. He does not orchestrate bad times in our lives, but He does work through them. Romans 2:4 tells us, "Or do you despise the riches of His goodness, forbearance, and longsuffering, not knowing that the goodness of God leads you to repentance?"

To illustrate, I submit this story for you to prayerfully think about:

A man had two sons named Billy and Jimmy. Billy was a healthy nine-year-old, but Jimmy needed a liver transplant to save his life. In the process of running tests on Jimmy, the doctors had told the dad that Billy's liver was an exact match for Jimmy. One day while Billy and his dad were out fishing, a storm began to rock the boat, and Billy fell out. Since Billy couldn't swim, he began to cry out to his father, who rushed to his side. However, once his father got to his side, he decided to allow Billy to drown so that the doctors could remove his liver and save Jimmy's life. What would we think of that father? We would probably charge him with murder. Yet don't we sometimes imply that God does the same thing?

A young Christian girl in our town died recently. At her funeral, several of her classmates accepted Jesus as their Lord because of the strong witness of this young woman's life. Several people commented that God allowed the death of that precious young lady to save those friends. Don't say that about my heavenly Father! Inadvertently, they were charging God with murder, because He had the ability to help but chose not to do so. They were also saying that the sacrifice of Jesus was not enough. They were implying that this young lady also had to be sacrificed to save her friends.

Sometimes we say things that sound good in difficult circumstances to relieve some of the suffering the family is feeling, but we should never put the blame on God! Satan is the one who "steals, kills and destroys" (John 10:10). God was merciful and made something good come of the situation but He didn't cause it to happen. In Matthew 7:9-11, Jesus says, "Or what man is there among you who, if his son asks for bread, will give him a stone? Or if he asks for a fish, will he give him a serpent? If you then, being evil, know how to give good gifts to your children, how much more will your Father who is in heaven give *good* things to those who ask Him" (emphasis added). Knowing that God loves us and desires the best for us is the only way for us to have the confidence (faith) to trust Him in everything.

Another way religion has broken down our confidence in God is by giving us the impression that God is in heaven just waiting for us to mess up. When we do, *wham!* Judgment cometh! Sometimes people also say, "God *is* going to get you for that." God is righteous and holy and has no communion with unrighteousness. But that is why He sent Jesus! First John 1:9 tells us that repentance is the path to righteousness. We all foul up from time to time, and God does render discipline if we fail to follow His Word and repent. However, when we *do* repent, we can restore our relationship with Him because we become righteous again through Jesus Christ. Occasionally, we become hard-hearted and will not repent. At those times, God will discipline us for our own good, just as a loving father will discipline his children (see Heb. 12:5-11). However, everything that God does for us—even discipline—is done in the light of His awesome love for each of us.

Now, since Jesus is called "the author and finisher of our faith" (Heb. 12:2), let us take a look at what He had to say about faith. In Matthew 8:5-10, we read how the servant of a centurion was healed:

> Now when Jesus had entered Capernaum, a centurion came to Him, pleading with Him, saying, "Lord, my servant is lying at home paralyzed, dreadfully tormented." And Jesus said to him, "I will come and heal him." The centurion answered and said, "Lord, I am not worthy that

You should come under my roof. But only speak a word, and my servant will be healed. For I also am a man under authority, having soldiers under me. And I say to this one, 'Go,' and he goes; and to another, 'Come,' and he comes; and to my servant, 'Do this,' and he does it." When Jesus heard it, He marveled, and said to those who followed, "Assuredly, I say to you, I have not found such *great* faith, not even in Israel!" (emphasis added).

This centurion told Jesus to just say the word and his servant would be healed. Jesus called that *great* faith. When we put complete confidence in the words of Jesus, we also have great faith. When we have great faith, we can expect the results this centurion received when Jesus told him in verse 13, "Go your way; and as you have believed, so let it be done for you." The Bible then says, "His servant was healed that same hour."

In contrast, Matthew 6:30-34 shows us how Jesus measured little faith:

Now if God so clothes the grass of the field, which today is, and tomorrow is thrown into the oven, will He not much more clothe you, O you of little faith? Therefore do not worry, saying, "What shall we eat" or "What shall we drink?" or "What shall we wear?" For after all these things the Gentiles seek. For your heavenly Father knows that you need all these things. But seek first the kingdom of God and His righteousness, and all these things shall be added to you. Therefore do not worry about tomorrow, for tomorrow will worry about its own things. Sufficient for the day is its own trouble.

Then, in Matthew 8:23-27, we read this story:

Now when He got into a boat, His disciples followed Him. And suddenly a great tempest arose on the sea, so that the boat was covered with the waves. But He was asleep. Then His disciples came to Him and awoke Him, saying, "Lord, save us! We are perishing!" But He said to them, "Why are you fearful, O you of little faith?" Then He arose and rebuked the winds and the sea, and there was a great calm. So the men marveled, saying, "Who can this be, that even the winds and the sea obey Him?"

Finally, in Matthew 14:30-31, we read the following:

When he [Peter] saw that the wind was boisterous, he was afraid; and beginning to sink he cried out, saying, "Lord, save me!" And immediately Jesus stretched out His hand and caught him, and said to him, "O you of little faith, why did you doubt?"

Jesus tells us that people display little faith when they worry (see Matt. 6:30), are fearful (see Matt. 8:26), or doubt (see Matt. 14:31). Each of these emotions or feelings exhibits a lack of confidence that God will do what He says He will do. If we are going to conquer worry, fear and doubt, we must develop faith in our lives. That level of faith is developed by "hearing and hearing by the Word of God" (Rom. 10:17) and then allowing the Word to renew our minds (see Rom. 12:1-2). God is gracious enough to give us a sufficient measure of faith to believe in Him, but we must read and listen to the anointed Word of God so that our faith can grow to become *great* faith.

As human beings, our actions are dictated by what our five senses (what we see, feel, hear, smell, and touch) tell us. When we are born again, our spirit is recreated into the likeness of God. Please do not misunderstand—we do not become God, but our spirits are recreated into God's image. God does not put any confidence in the flesh; therefore, we should not put confidence in the flesh but in what God says in His Word. Romans 8:5-6 says, "For those who live according to the flesh set their minds on the things of the flesh, but those who live according to the Spirit, the things of the Spirit. For to be carnally minded is death [separation from God], but to be spiritually minded is life and peace."

There will be situations that arise in our lives that will fail to make sense. We won't be able to figure them out. However, when we realize that the promises of God are backed up by God's character, we can believe in our hearts that what God says is true. This will enable us to then disregard what our senses are telling us and what Satan is tempting us to believe. That is why God is pleased when we display faith. It shows our confidence in His character and in His promise that He will never leave us or forsake us (see Deut. 31:6).

Before my first mission in Desert Storm, I was scared—very scared. I had made all the preparations, read all the promises of God's protection and knew that there were plenty of people back home praying for me. However, as I was checking over my aircraft, my knees were shaking, my heart was pounding and a little voice inside my head was crying out, *This will be your last day on earth!*

As I flew my aircraft toward the battle zone, I rehearsed my attack profile over and over. When the missiles started flying and the anti-aircraft shells started exploding around me, I relied on my training to escape the attacks and then proceeded to complete my assigned mission by dropping my load of bombs on the designated target. As I flew away from the target area and away from the threat, a sense of relief and praise flooded my cockpit. I came to the realization that because I had trained properly and had God's protection, I did not have anything to fear. From that moment on, I was never afraid again. In fact, one entry of my daily diary says that I needed to be careful not to become too complacent about the threat or I might do something stupid that would needlessly place my wingman or myself in harm's way.

Having God, the Author and Creator of this universe, living inside us has tremendous advantages. However, we must meditate on His Word to develop our faith in His infallible character and His awesome love for us. Only then will the full effect of His existence be manifested in our lives. Ephesians 3:20 tells us that He "is able to do exceedingly, abundantly above all that we can ask or think, according to the power that works in us." When the Word produces faith in our lives, we have the power to overcome the world. First John 5: 4-5 says, "For whatever is born of God overcomes the world. And this is the victory that has overcome the world—our faith. Who is he who overcomes the world, but he who believes that Jesus is the Son of God." Let us resolve to be people of faith—people who overcome!

CHAPTER 6

THE WEAPON OF PRAYER

IF A GROUP of Christians were asked what is one of their most important daily tasks, prayer would probably be one of the top answers. However, while the majority of Christians understand the need for prayer, very few understand why prayer is a necessity. As a result, many Christians use prayer incorrectly. Prayer is simply the way in which we communicate with our heavenly Father. It is not something we do when we can't think of anything else to do or as a means of asking our spiritual "Santa Claus" for what we desire.

As Christians, we must realize that prayer is one of the most powerful spiritual weapons at our disposal. Through prayer, we can boldly come before the Creator of the universe for one-on-one communication. Through this communication, we can get instruction about how we should conduct ourselves on this earth as well as receive the things we need. Without prayer, our ability to accomplish things for God is hindered, because we end up doing these things in our own strength instead of using God's wisdom and direction. It is essential for us to master our arsenal of prayer weapons, because it is through the use of these weapons of prayer that we can unlock the awesome power of our Father in heaven to change any situation we may encounter.

James 5:16 tells us, "Confess your trespasses to one another, and pray for one another, that you may be healed. The effective, fervent prayer of a righteous man avails much." It is not just praying that benefits us; it is the *effective, fervent prayer* that is beneficial to us. To have an effective prayer life, we must build it on God's solid foundation, for otherwise it won't stand the test of time or weather the storms that come its way. Employing an effective prayer life will activate God's power enabling His will to be done on earth in any situation.

There are two foundational stones that must be in place before we can have a good prayer life. The first foundational stone is the realization that God is limited on this earth (only because He has limited Himself by His Word) until we, His children, pray. The second foundational stone is an understanding of each type of prayer and an ability to use those types of prayers effectively. Understanding these principles and implementing them into our prayer life will dramatically increase the effectiveness of our prayers.

In order to lay the first foundational stone, we must understand why God's power is limited on earth. To receive this understanding, we must go back to the beginning. God created man perfect and sinless. Genesis 1:27 says, "So God created man in His own image; in the image of God He created him; male and female He created them. Then God blessed them and God said to them, 'Be fruitful and multiply; fill the earth and subdue it; have dominion over the fish of the sea, over the birds of the air, and over every living thing that moves on the earth.'" God created man in His image and gave him dominion over the things on this earth.

Life in the Garden of Eden was wonderful and peaceful. Man tended the Garden and enjoyed face-to-face fellowship with God during the cool of the day. There wasn't any sickness or disease in the Garden, thorns and thistles didn't grow there, and, although the Bible doesn't specifically state this, I believe there weren't any mosquitoes or fleas either! Man was created with God-given dominion, and he was created to live forever. What happened? Man was deceived by Satan and died spiritually. Once sin entered into man, God no longer had the ability to fellowship with him face-to-face, because if sinful man looked upon God who was righteous and holy, he would have died instantly. We can see the result of man having seen God's face when He told Moses in Exodus 33:20, "You cannot see My face; for no man shall see Me, and live." Once man sinned, communication with God had to occur spiritually (God communicating through our spirit).

The problem is that man's spirit is dead (separated from God) and has to be reborn (by accepting the sacrifice Jesus made for us) in order to have the ability to communicate with God. In the Old Testament, when men and women believed God, it was counted to them as righteousness (right standing with God), which gave them the ability to hear God and be heard by Him. When Jesus died and was raised victorious from the grave, He bridged the gap between man and God by paying the price for sin. Once we accept the sacrifice Jesus made for us, we put on His righteousness, which gives us the ability to spiritually meet God through prayer. We still cannot look at God face-to-face in the physical sense, because our flesh has not yet been redeemed. However, prayer is the avenue that God has provided for us so that we can freely communicate with Him. Through prayer, we can talk with God as any child talks with his father. Prayer gives us an avenue to tell God how much we love Him, solicit His instruction on how we should live our lives on this earth, and express our needs, concerns, fears, and desires to Him.

Something else happened at the fall of man that thereafter prevented God from moving as He willed on this earth. In 2 Corinthians 4:3-4, Paul says, "But even if our gospel is veiled, it is veiled to those who are perishing, whose minds the *god of this age* has blinded, who do not believe, lest the light of the gospel of the glory of Christ, who is the image of God, should shine on them" (emphasis added). Notice that Satan is called "the god of this age." In Luke 4, we can read about the temptation of Jesus. I want to emphasize verses five through eight:

> Then the devil, taking Him up on a high mountain, showed Him all the kingdoms of the world in a moment of time. And the devil said to Him, "All this authority I will give You, and their glory; for this has been delivered to me, and I give it to whomever I wish. Therefore, if You will worship before me, all will be Yours." And Jesus answered and said to him, "Get behind Me, Satan! For it is written, 'You shall worship the Lord your God, and Him only you shall serve.'"

Satan told Jesus that the authority of all the kingdoms of the earth had been delivered to him. How was that authority delivered to him? Satan deceived Adam and stole the authority that God had given to him. God intended for man to rule and reign on the earth; however, when Adam committed high treason against God, Satan became the god of this world and gained authority over all the kingdoms of the earth.

Some people believe Satan was lying when he told Jesus that he had the authority to give Him all the kingdoms of the world. However, the facts stated in 2 Corinthians 4:4, Luke 4:5-8 and John 16:11 reveal that Satan was telling Jesus the truth. Jesus is God who became flesh. He knew where He came from. "He was in the beginning with God and all things were made through Him" (John 1:2 3). Jesus knew everything that had transpired between God and the devil and what had happened between Adam and the devil. So, if Satan had lied to Jesus, Jesus would have known that it was a lie. If Jesus knew it was a lie, He would not have been tempted to accept the devil's proposition, because there wouldn't have been any foundation to the devil's temptation. However, the Bible says Jesus *was* tempted, so there had to be truth to the devil's statement.

Let's say, for example, that an acquaintance said he would give you one million dollars to quit your job and go into business with him. Now, if you knew that he lived in a shack and didn't have a penny to his name, you wouldn't be tempted to leave your good job for his phony offer. On the other hand, if a well-known billionaire showed you several million dollars and then offered it to you on the condition that you would steal technology from your company, you might be tempted, because you saw the money. Unless there is substance behind an offer, it will not be a temptation. That is why we know Satan was telling Jesus the truth when he told Him he had all the authority over the kingdoms of this world. Jesus Himself called the devil the ruler of this world when He said in John 16:11, "Because the ruler of this world is judged." In the context of this passage, He had to be talking about the devil.

To better explain the concept of Satan being the god of this world and having authority over all of the kingdoms of this world, let's say that a chief executive officer (CEO) of a corporation was going on an extended trip. Before he left, he gave the president of the corporation full authority to operate the company while he was gone. During the CEO's absence, the president decided to sell a very lucrative piece of property that the company owned. After the CEO returned and found out about the deal, he became angry because he had expansion plans for the property that had been sold.

Now, if the CEO went to the people who purchased the land and asked for it back based on the fact the president should not have sold them the property, do you think they would give it back? No way! They would show the CEO the legal document with the president's signature transferring ownership to them. They might remind the CEO that if he did want it back, he would have to pay for it. Until he did though, he had no authority to be on the property or do anything to the property.

That is exactly what happened when Adam sold out to the devil. Satan gained authority over man and the kingdoms of this world. God was on the outside looking in. He is all-powerful, but He didn't have any authority in the kingdoms of this world. God could not do what He wanted to in the earth because if He did, He would have gone back on His Word that gave man dominion (the ability to make decisions) on the earth.

The consequence of having Satan become the god of this world is that everyone who lives in this world (his kingdom) is subject to him.

Romans 6:17 tells us, "Though you were slaves of sin, yet you obeyed from the heart that form of doctrine to which you were delivered." Before we accepted Jesus, we were slaves to the devil. Ephesians 2:1-3 explains it this way: "And you He made alive, who were dead in trespasses and sins, in which you once walked according to the course of this world, according to the prince of the power of the air, the spirit who now works in the sons of disobedience, among whom also we all once conducted ourselves in the lusts of our flesh, fulfilling the desires of the flesh and of the mind, and were by nature children of wrath, just as the others."

When the Jewish leaders came to Jesus to challenge His authority, He let them know whom they served. In John 8:44, He said, "You are of your father the devil, and the desires of your father you want to do. He was a murderer from the beginning, and does not stand in the truth, because there is no truth in him. When he speaks a lie, he speaks from his own resources, for he is a liar and the father of it." As long as this world is under Satan's authority, it will naturally move further away from God. Even creation itself was subjected to the corruption. In Romans 8:19-22, Paul states, "For the earnest expectation of the creation eagerly waits for the revealing of the sons of God. For the creation was subjected to futility, not willingly, but because of Him who subjected it in hope; because the creation itself also will be delivered from the bondage of corruption into the glorious liberty of the children of God. For we know that the whole creation groans and labors with birth pangs together until now."

After the Fall, humans were in an awful situation because they were now subject to the authority of Satan. Jesus came to change this hopeless situation. He paid the ultimate price to redeem mankind and then defeated Satan, allowing Him to take back the authority Satan had gained by deceiving Adam. When we accept Jesus' sacrifice and make Him Lord of our lives, we are spiritually transferred from Satan's kingdom into God's kingdom. First Peter 2:9 tells us, "But you are a chosen generation, a royal priesthood, a holy nation, His own special people, that you may proclaim the praises of Him who called you out of darkness into His marvelous light." We have been called out of darkness. Praise God!

God didn't stop with the calling; He actually transferred us out of the world's darkness. Colossians 1:13 says, "He has delivered us from the power of darkness and conveyed us into the kingdom of the Son of His love." The good news about being a Christian is that we are no longer subject to the god of this world. He isn't our master any longer. In addition, since we have been transferred to God's kingdom, we can enjoy the benefits stated in 1 John 5:4: "For whatever is born of God overcomes the world. And this is the victory that has overcome the world—our faith."

Prayer empowers us to fight the spiritual forces at work in this world. Take a look at 2 Corinthians 4:3-4 once again. Satan has a legal right to blind the eyes of those in his kingdom and prevent them from seeing the light of the gospel. However, even though Satan has that right, Jesus states that we have the right to bring these people into God's kingdom: "And Jesus came and spoke to them, saying, 'All authority has been given to Me in heaven and on earth. Go therefore and make disciples of all the nations, baptizing them in the name of the Father and of the Son and of the Holy Spirit, teaching them to observe all things that I have commanded you; and lo, I am with you always, even to the end of the age'" (Matt. 28:18-20). So even though Satan is the god of this world, we are commissioned to go into his world and get people out of his kingdom!

This process is not automatic. We must use the authority given to us by Jesus to bind Satan (see Matt. 18:19) and prevent him from blinding lost people's eyes, which then allows God to present Himself to them. Mark 16:17-18 tells us what signs should follow as we make disciples: "And these signs will follow those who believe: In My name they will cast out demons; they will speak with new tongues; they will take up serpents; and if they drink anything deadly, it will by no means hurt them; they will lay hands on the sick, and they will recover." When people are sick, our authority gives us the ability to ask for the power of God to heal them. If there are other needs, we must be ready to act, because *we* are the ones who have been called to make disciples of all nations. Through prayer, we receive the instructions necessary to accomplish this great commission. As we communicate with God through prayer, He directs our feet to go where He couldn't go before, uses our hands to work where He couldn't work before, and uses our mouth to proclaim His Son as King of Kings and Lord of Lords to all mankind.

God is love and is all-powerful and all knowing. However, He will never violate His Word. Even though God wants to move on our behalf, He cannot do it until a person in right standing with Him (who is righteous) asks Him to move. The only way for us to be righteous is by applying 1 John 1:9: "If we confess our sins, He is faithful and just to forgive us our sins and to cleanse us from all unrighteousness." Once we have cleansed ourselves of all unrighteousness, we become righteous. 1 John 3:7 tells us that if we practice righteousness, we are righteous and just as He (Jesus) is righteous. When one of God's children who in right standing with Him asks Him for something, it gives Him the legal right to move in this world system (Satan's domain), because He is moving on behalf of one of His children.

Our enemy, the devil, is very aware of the power of prayer. He understands that through prayer, we put ourselves in a position to receive the guidance necessary to develop our faith into "overcoming faith" (see Rom. 10:17). He realizes that when we ask God for something and believe that we will receive (see Mark 11:23-24), God is free to move the way He wants in this world system. Day and night, the devil and his demons are looking for avenues to attack. That is why Paul wrote in 1 Thessalonians 5:16-18 to: "Rejoice always, pray without ceasing, in everything give thanks; for this is the will of God in Christ Jesus for you." Jesus told us in Luke 21:36, "Watch therefore, and pray always that you may be counted worthy to escape all these things that will come to pass, and to stand before the Son of Man." We are instructed to pray all the time but that is difficult to accomplish because our flesh, under the control of its god, the devil, will think of any and every excuse for us not to pray. Satan has to keep us out of a position in which we can receive revelation from God because once we ask in faith, God has every right to do His will on this earth just as He does in heaven (see Matt. 6:10). When that happens, Satan's schemes are thwarted and his capabilities are rendered useless.

In 2 Corinthians 5:17, Paul states that once we decide to make Jesus the Lord of our life, we "become a new creation." Even though we might look the same on the outside, we aren't the same beings as we were before. We are no longer slaves to sin. Our past is forgiven, and our spirit is reborn into the likeness of God's Spirit. We become God's children! Jesus' victory over Satan gives us the ability to overcome everything the flesh has to offer, including temptation, sickness, poverty, doubt, fear and depression. So, even though we still physically live in this world, we have been enabled to overcome every hindrance that can interfere with our ability to pray without ceasing.

Throughout the Bible, we find promise after promise of God's provision for us. Ephesians 1:3 says, "Blessed be the God and Father of our Lord Jesus Christ, who has blessed us with every spiritual blessing in the heavenly places in Christ." Psalm 1:3 says, "He shall be like a tree planted by the rivers of water, that brings forth its fruit in its season, whose leaf also shall not wither; and whatever he does shall prosper." Second Peter 1:3 tells us, "As His divine power has given to us *all things* that pertain to life and godliness, through the knowledge of Him who called us by glory and virtue" (emphasis added). Everything we need has been given to us, but we must receive what has been given in order to manifest it in our lives. Prayer enables us to find out from God how to direct our faith to bring what we need from the spiritual realm to a place where we experience it with our physical senses.

Once we realize the need for continual prayer, we must put our knowledge of the second foundational stone into action in order to have an effective prayer life. We must recognize that there are different types of prayer that should be used at different times and in different circumstances. Putting these prayers into action will move God on our behalf to miraculously change the world around us. The rest of this chapter will give a brief description of the different types of prayer, which include praise, confession, intercession, petition, protection, and direction.

The precious blood of God's Son bought salvation for us. Because God loved us so much, we have the ability to love Him. This love should be demonstrated first by keeping His commandments (see John 14:15) and then by praising Him for His marvelous deeds. Psalm 34:1-3 says, "I will bless the LORD at all times; his praise shall continually be in my mouth. My soul shall make its boast in the LORD; the humble shall hear of it and be glad. Oh, magnify the LORD with me, and let us exalt His name together." David also tells us in Psalm 69:30, "I will praise the name of God with a song, and will magnify Him with thanksgiving."

If a person did something wonderful for us, our natural response would be to thank that person and then praise him or her for helping us. Spiritually, God has done *the most* wonderful thing for us by giving Jesus as a sacrifice for our sin. Praise is simply pouring our heart out to God to acknowledge how awesome He is and giving resounding appreciation for who He is. Praise puts a voice to our thankfulness for what He has done for us in the past, how He is presently working in our lives, and how He will continue to do glorious things for us in the future.

In Psalm 92:1-4, the psalmist proclaims, "It is good to give thanks to the LORD, and to sing praises to Your name, O Most High; to declare Your loving kindness in the morning, and Your faithfulness every night, on an instrument of ten strings, on the lute, and on the harp, with harmonious sound. For You, LORD, have made me glad through Your work; I will triumph in the works of Your hands." Psalm 147:1-7 says, "Praise the LORD! For it is good to sing praises to our God; for it is pleasant, and praise is beautiful. The LORD builds up Jerusalem; he gathers together the outcasts of Israel. He heals the brokenhearted and binds up their wounds. He counts the number of the stars; he calls them all by name. Great is our LORD, and mighty in power; his understanding is infinite. The LORD lifts up the humble; he casts the wicked down to the ground. Sing to the LORD with thanksgiving; sing praises on the harp to our God."

Praise also displays a tremendous faith in God. When Paul and Silas were thrown into prison, they did not moan and complain. They chose to praise God, which displayed their awesome confidence in the almighty God and their confidence that He was in control of the situation. Likewise, when we are faced with life's difficulties, our praise exhibits our confidence in God. As we focus on the awesome attributes of God, the things that we are going through will be minimized by His goodness and power. In any situation, when we praise God, we can expect to be delivered just as Paul and Silas were. When we praise God in good situations and difficult situations, we are acknowledging that the Father, Son and Holy Spirit have first place in our lives. When God is first, we are in direct fellowship with Him, and His miraculous power can freely flow in our lives to change any situation we may encounter—positive or negative—into something that will bring Him glory.

The prayer of praise does something else. When Jesus met the woman at the well in John 4, He told her that "those who worship Him [God] must worship in spirit and truth" (v. 24). True praise can only be done in the Spirit. We are empowered to express our praise for God here on earth when our spirit yields to His Spirit. In Matthew 12:28, Jesus stated, "But if I cast out demons by the Spirit of God, surely the kingdom of God has come upon you." Where the Spirit is, there is the kingdom of God. Now look at the Lord's Prayer in Matthew 6: 9-10: "Our Father in heaven, hallowed be Your name. Your kingdom come, Your will be done on earth as it is in heaven." Praise moves us into the Spirit, which brings the kingdom of God and enables Him to perform His will *on earth* as it is in heaven.

The prayer of praise is vitally important. However, there are other types of prayer that are equally important. One of these is the prayer of confession, for without the forgiveness of sins, none of our other prayers will be heard. It is important to remember that we have to be righteous (in right standing with God) in order to communicate with God, who is righteous. If there is sin in our lives, we become unrighteous. We all face this problem, because the Bible says that we all sin (see 1 John 1:8) The good news is that we can be forgiven (see 1 John 1:9). The prayer of confession is what we use to acknowledge our sin and accept God's forgiveness.

When we confess our sins and repent, all unrighteousness is removed from us and we become righteous again. When God forgives, He also forgets. Ps 103:12 says, "As far as the east is from the west, so far has He removed our transgressions from us." In Jeremiah 31:34, God tells us, "For I will forgive their iniquity, and their sin I will remember no more." In God's eyes, once we ask for and receive forgiveness, it is as if we have never sinned. Too often, the devil will remind us of something in our past for which we have been forgiven and makes us once again feel the need to come crawling to God to ask for forgiveness again. When we come to God in those situations, He asks, "What are you talking about? I do not remember you doing that!" Jesus' sacrifice made it easy for us. We cannot let the devil continually hold us in bondage to past sins. We are free! Remember, "Therefore if the Son makes you free, you shall be free indeed" (John 8:36). First John 3:7 takes our thinking one step further when it states that we are righteous just as He is righteous. Because of what Jesus did for us, we can "boldly come to the throne of grace" (Heb. 4:16) and receive the things we need just as if Jesus Himself were coming to the Father.

Another type of prayer is intercessory prayer. Intercessory prayer is going before the Father on behalf of someone else. All of us deserve the judgment of God. However, Jesus was willing to become our substitute, and now He is the One who steps in and tells the Father, "Let My sacrifice be sufficient for their unrighteousness." Just as Jesus intercedes for us (Hebrews 7:25 says, "He always lives to make intercession for them"), we need to do the same for our brothers and sisters in Christ as well as for people who don't know the Lord. Intercession allows God to move on the merits of the one praying instead of on the righteousness of the one in need.

A perfect example of someone interceding for another is the story of Stephen, who interceded for those who stoned him. In Acts 7:59-60 it says, "And they stoned Stephen as he was calling on God and saying, 'Lord Jesus, receive my spirit.' Then he knelt down and cried out with a loud voice, 'Lord, do not charge them with this sin.' And when he had said this, he fell asleep." Stephen asked God for mercy for those who were stoning him. We should follow his example by interceding for our brothers and sisters in Jesus as well as for those who might persecute us. James 5:16 tells us, "The effective, fervent prayer of a righteous man avails much." In certain situations, a righteous person (one whose sins have been forgiven) has the ability to bring about God's miraculous power to heal or forgive when there should be judgment. This principle is very evident when Abraham interceded for Sodom in Genesis 18:16-33. First Peter 4:8 says, "And above all things have fervent love for one another, for 'love will cover a multitude of sins.'" When we love people enough to go to the Father on their behalf, God is able to move when it was not possible before.

Seeking the heart of God is another form of prayer that is done by a person or persons called into the ministry of intercession. God specifically calls and equips these types of intercessors. Ezekiel was one such intercessor who was called by God to pray for Israel. In Ezekiel 3:17, God says, "Son of man, I have made you a watchman for the house of Israel; therefore hear a word from My mouth, and give them warning from Me." Those who are called into this ministry have a very sensitive heart, are very passionate about what they do, and have a constant burden to spend time with God. They are content where God has put them, even though they are rarely seen. Every ministry needs this type of intercessor praying for them. These intercessors are specifically called to fight spiritual battles and relieve some of the burden from the person in charge so that he or she can hear from God. You will not find a successful minister of the gospel that does not have a group of intercessors praying for him or her.

Intercession is one of the highest callings that we can have. Whether it is a one-time event to pray for someone or a lifetime calling from God, intercession connects us with the heart of God. God is love, and when we seek Him on behalf of others, we hook into that love. There is nothing on this earth or in this life that can compare to the times spent in true intercession. The ability to flow in the love of our Father through intercession gives us a closeness and freedom of expression that cannot occur in any other setting.

If you have never interceded before, spend some time with God on behalf of someone else. Set aside a time when you will disregard your desires and wants in order to minister to God and pray for the needs of someone else. When you do, be prepared to sense God's presence like never before, because when you minister to Him and pray for others, you are touching the very heart of God.

We all have needs in this life. The prayer of petition is a type of prayer that we can pray to ask God to meet those needs. God established His covenant of provision with us when He appropriated Jesus' sacrifice to our lives. Matthew 6:8 tells us, "Therefore do not be like them [the hypocrites]. For your Father knows the things you have need of before you ask Him." Not only does God know what we need, He also has provided *everything* we need. Philippians 4:19-20 tells us, "And my God shall supply *all your need* according to His riches in glory by Christ Jesus" (emphasis added).

It is vital to understand that even though we have a covenant with God to meet our every need, His provision is not automatic. We cannot stop short at just believing that God will supply our need; we must also put our belief into action when we ask for the things we need. Until we ask, our God-given provision will stay in the spiritual realm and never reach the physical realm. Once we know our covenant of provision, we must then have the faith to receive the things that have been provided by God. Mark 11:24 reveals this truth: "Therefore I say to you, whatever things you ask when you pray, believe that you receive them, and you will have them." Through the prayer of petition, we acknowledge the covenant between God and ourselves and then receive the benefits our covenant provides.

If God knows what we need and has provided all we need, why are so many Christians *in* need? Hosea 4:6 says, "My people are destroyed for lack of knowledge." For the prayer of petition to be effective, we must be asking God for things that are consistent with His Word. First John 5:14-15 tells us, "Now this is the confidence that we have in Him, that if we ask anything according to His will, He hears us. And if we know that He hears us, whatever we ask, we know that we have the petitions that we have asked of Him."

In addition, when we pray the prayer of petition, we must not allow doubt to enter into our prayers. James 1:6-8 makes it clear what doubt brings: "But let him ask in faith, with no doubting, for he who doubts is like a wave of the sea driven and tossed by the wind. For let not that man suppose that he will receive anything from the Lord; he is a double-minded man, unstable in all his ways." We cannot pray the prayer of petition using a promise found in His Word and then add an "if it be Your will" to the end of the request. Such words display doubt. Remember, God's Word, recorded in the Bible, *is* His will for our lives.

When we say, "if it be Your will," we are subconsciously giving God an out. When we do not immediately receive something we are praying for, it becomes easier for us to say, "Well, I guess it wasn't God's will for me to have it," instead of continuing to believe His Word and standing firm until we do receive. Remember, if we find a promise in the Word, we can pray with the assurance that we will receive what we are requesting. If something we need is included in the Word, we can rest assured that *it is God's will for us to have it.* Adding, "if it be Your will" to the end of our prayers reveals the fact that we doubt God will give us the things for which we are asking.

I want to reemphasize that the prayer of petition is not a shot in the dark in which we hope we will receive something from God. Instead, it is an acknowledgement of our covenant with God Almighty and a faith-filled proclamation that we will receive those things we are asking for. When we use the prayer of petition, we demonstrate our belief that God is our source and trust that He will provide the things we need.

Another type of prayer is the prayer for direction. This type of prayer is used to get God's guidance about different situations that we encounter in life. These prayers would be for things such as what school to attend, where to work, whom to marry, and so forth. This is the only type of prayer that should include the words "if it be Your will," as we won't be able to find answers to these types of questions in Scripture. Jesus used this type of prayer in the Garden of Gethsemane when He asked the Father if He could forego all the pain and agony He was about to endure. Thank God He yielded to His Father's will instead of His own!

As we develop our communication and dependence on the Lord, He will constantly update us on His will for our lives. Although most of us like to know everything *now*, we typically do not get the whole picture of God's will for our lives at one time. God, in His infinite wisdom, knows that we can only handle a little bit at a time, so He only lets us see bits and pieces. Only when we are mature enough or in a position to receive will God reveal different parts of His will for our lives. This is clarified in James 4:13-15: "Come now, you who say, 'Today or tomorrow we will go to such and such a city, spend a year there, buy and sell, and make a profit'; whereas you do not know what will happen tomorrow. For what is your life? It is even a vapor that appears for a little time and then vanishes away. Instead you ought to say, 'If the Lord wills, we shall live and do this or that.'" We should constantly be open to receive new instruction from the Lord. This builds dependence and a deep trust in our heavenly Father. Receiving constant updates from the Lord about His will for our lives is the only way we can be assured that we are walking a life that is pleasing to Him and that will be blessed by Him.

Recently, I was praying about why we do not receive more of the plans God has for our lives. I sensed God telling me the primary reason was because we would kill the plans with the words of our mouths before we had developed the faith to support those plans. If God told us everything He had for us before we had the faith to believe it, the devil would be able to steal some of those things from us. We shouldn't worry about the details of the things God has told us to do. We just need to develop our lives to the point that He can fully entrust us with His plan.

Just as all of our needs have already been provided, our covenant with God already provides protection for our families and ourselves. The prayer of protection, which is another type of prayer in our arsenal, is really just a confession of protection. Look at Psalm 91 and Deuteronomy 28:1-14. God's covenant to protect is complete. However, just as our provision is not automatic, our protection is also not automatic. We are required to appropriate His protection through prayer by acknowledging the promises found in Scripture and then stand on those promises regardless of what our senses might tell us.

Satan cannot touch us when we are taking refuge under God's wing. Proverbs 3:21-26 shows us the confidence in which we should walk: "My son, let them not depart from your eyes—keep sound wisdom and discretion; So they will be life to your soul and grace to your neck. Then you will walk safely in your way, and your foot will not stumble. When you lie down, you will not be afraid; yes, you will lie down and your sleep will be sweet. *Do* not be afraid of sudden terror, nor of trouble from the wicked when it comes; For the LORD will be your confidence, and will keep your foot from being caught." The biblical confidence in God's protection doesn't come with a casual acquaintance with God. Only through constant communication (such as prayer) can we come to the place in which we trust Him fully to perform the things He has written in His Word.

There are occasions when we do not know how to pray. These occasions might come about as a result of not knowing how or what to pray or because of an unknown churning inside our spirit. God gave us the Holy Spirit to help in these situations. In Ephesians 6:18, Paul encourages us to pray "always with all prayer and supplication in the Spirit, being watchful to this end with all perseverance and supplication for all the saints." The Holy Spirit can pray the perfect will of God through us.

In 1 Corinthians 14, Paul wrote to the church of Corinth about spiritual gifts. In verses two through thirteen, he told the Corinthians about speaking in tongues. Then in verses fourteen and fifteen, he spoke about praying in tongues, saying, "For if I pray in a tongue, my spirit prays but my understanding is unfruitful. What is the conclusion then? I will pray with the spirit, and I will pray with the understanding." We are encouraged to pray with the Spirit (in an unknown tongue) and with the understanding. When we pray in an unknown tongue, our minds may not understand what we are saying, but we will be praying the perfect will of our Father because our recreated spirit is telling our mouths what to pray. There have been many times in my life when I've been awakened during the night to pray for someone. Without the slightest idea of the problem, I would pray as the Spirit gave me utterance. On several of these occasions, the one for whom I was praying later told me about being delivered from a terrible situation.

Praying in the Spirit is one way we can pray without ceasing. When we do not know how to pray, we can yield to the Spirit and let Him give utterance to how we should pray. Romans 8:26-27 says, "Likewise the Spirit also helps in our weaknesses. For we do not know what we should pray for as we ought, but the Spirit Himself makes intercession for us with groanings which cannot be uttered. Now He who searches the hearts knows what the mind of the Spirit is, because He makes intercession for the saints according to the will of God."

Praying in the spirit has the additional advantage in building our faith. Look at Jude (that little book right before Revelation), verse 20: "But you, beloved, building yourselves up on your most holy faith, praying in the Holy Spirit." Praying in the Holy Spirit builds our faith. The reason this is possible is because faith comes from hearing the spoken word of God (see Rom. 10:17). When we pray in the Spirit, we pray what our recreated spirit hears from God! If you have never experienced this wonderful gift that God gives to every believer, ask for it now! When you pray in the Sprit, you will sense a greater power in yourself to do what God has called you to do.

If there are any other questions about prayer, we only need to go to the One who is the expert to get our instruction. Jesus told us to pray this way in Matthew 6:9-13: "Our Father in heaven, hallowed be Your name. Your kingdom come. Your will be done on earth as it is in heaven. Give us this day our daily bread. And forgive us our debts, as we forgive our debtors. And do not lead us into temptation, but deliver us from the evil one. For Yours is the kingdom and the power and the glory forever. Amen." Notice that Jesus started this model prayer with praise. He then asked for God's kingdom to come and His will to be done on this earth as it is in heaven. Jesus knew that in order to achieve the coming of God's kingdom and to have His will done on this earth, His people would have to pray it into existence. The same thing is true in asking for "our daily bread"—we already have what we need, but we still are required to pray for it. Jesus then included a prayer for forgiveness and a prayer for protection. If we are going to walk as Jesus walked (see 1 John 2:6), we must learn to pray as Jesus prayed.

I hope that as you have read about the reasons we must pray, you have sensed the immense importance of prayer. Our ability to communicate directly with God is the primary reason prayer is one of the most powerful weapons at our disposal. Prayer must be constant, biblically based, and done in love. Everything is possible through prayer, and nothing significant will be accomplished without it. We are responsible to master and constantly use the weapons of prayer if we are going to rescue men and women from the kingdom of darkness. God has already done His part by empowering us to fulfill His great commission. Now it is time to do our part! *Pray!*

CHAPTER 7

LOVE: GOD'S ULTIMATE WEAPONS MANAGEMENT SYSTEM

BECAUSE THE F-16 is a multi-role fighter, it carries weapons used against ground targets and weapons used against enemy aircraft. For use against ground targets, the F-16 carries general-purpose bombs (500 or 2,000 pounds), Maverick missiles, cluster bomb units (CBU's), smart bombs or HARM missiles (used against surface-to-air missile sites), or a number of other varieties of weaponry. As mentioned earlier, the F-16 also carries the AAMRAM and AIM-9 missiles for employment against air targets and an internal Gatlin gun, which can be used against both ground and air targets. On any mission, the F-16 can be loaded with a wide array of artillery for use against both air-to-air and air-to-ground targets.

To manage all these weapons, the F-16 uses a computer called the Stores Management System, or SMS. The SMS keeps an inventory of the weapons onboard the aircraft and defines the parameters under which those weapons will be released. By using the SMS to precisely control the artillery on board the F-16, the pilot can increase the accuracy of each weapon, which optimizes the effectiveness of each mission. Even though the F-16 might be loaded with an awesome amount of deadly firepower, if the SMS fails, the aircraft will be very limited in the ways it can deliver its weapons.

As Christians, we have at our disposal a wide variety of spiritual weapons for use in different situations. The potential force of these weapons is awesome, but we must have a system like the F-16's SMS in our lives to control the delivery of those spiritual weapons. First Corinthians 13:1-3,13 tells us what that system is:

Though I speak with the tongues of men and of angels, but have not love, I have become sounding brass or a clanging cymbal. And though I have the gift of prophecy, and understand all mysteries and all knowledge, and though I have all faith, so that I could remove mountains, but have not love, I am nothing. And though I bestow all my goods to feed the poor, and though I give my body to be burned, but have not love, it profits me nothing....And now abide faith, hope, love, these three; but the greatest of these is love.

Love is the ultimate management tool God has given to us to increase the effectiveness of our spiritual weapons. Even though we possess a powerful spiritual arsenal, without love managing the spiritual weapons available to us, the success we have while engaging our enemy will be minimal.

Every spiritual weapon that we have comes from God. Look at 1 John 4:7-8: "Beloved, let us love one another, for love is of God; and everyone who loves is born of God and knows God. He who does not love does not know God, for *God is love*" (emphasis added). God is love. We cannot separate anything He does from love, because that is what and who He is. Every weapon is given to us because God loves us, and because He gives them, every weapon has love as its principle part. Therefore, to work properly, every spiritual weapon given by God must be used in love.

It is important to get a basic understanding of God's love. There are different words translated as love in the New Testament, but when the Bible talks about God's love, it uses the word *agape*. Agape is different than how we understand love. We say we love old movies and hot dogs. Most of time, we love things or people because they bring pleasure to us. God's love, or agape love, is not like that.

There are three characteristics that differentiate agape love from other types of love. First, agape love is a love by decision. When God created man, He already made the decision to love man. It did not matter what man did, does or ever will do. God's decision to love man was eternal. Second, agape love has a component of action associated with the words. "For God so loved the world that He gave" (John 3:16). "But God demonstrates His own love towards us, in that while we were still sinners, Christ died for us" (Rom. 5:8). Love has the action of giving associated with it. The third characteristic of agape love is that it raises the object loved to the highest position possible. God loved His Son and seated Him at His right hand. Ephesians 2:4-6 says, "But God, who is rich in mercy, because of His great love with which He loved us, even when we were dead in trespasses, made us alive together with Christ (by grace you have been saved), and raised us up together, and made us sit together in heavenly places in Christ Jesus."

If we are going to love as God loves, we must filter the use of the spiritual weapons He gave us through agape love. To illustrate this point, think about the spiritual weapons mentioned in the previous chapters. When separated from love, the weapon of the Word becomes legalistic and full of religion. John 1:14 tells us, "The Word became flesh and dwelt among us." Jesus is God's Word with flesh. Jesus was sent because God "so loved the world" (John 3:16). Jesus also said in John 10:30, "I and My Father are one." So, if God is love, then Jesus is love; and if Jesus is love, then the Word is love. When we accept the sacrifice Jesus made for us, we are made into a new creation. We are set free from the bondage of sin. It is the Word, working through love, which keeps us free. When the Word is used against our spiritual enemies, it is Jesus who comes against those enemies. When Jesus (love exemplified) comes against our enemies on our behalf, we can never fail, because "love never fails" (1 Cor. 13:8).

Unfortunately, religion has taken this truth, removed God's love out of equation, and twisted how we use the Word. Jesus told us in John 14:15, "If you love Me, keep My commandments." When we say we love Jesus, we are saying that we love the Word, which is Jesus. Therefore, if we do not do what His Word says, we do not love Him (John 14:24). Religion has taken this principle of keeping His commandments and created a list of "don't do" and "can't do" that have nothing to do with the Word.

When taken outside of the realm of love, the Word is binding and condemning, because no one can keep it completely. Too often, the Church takes commandments and makes laws out of them without imparting the love of God into those laws. For example, the Bible tells us not to be fornicators or adulterers. Some religious groups have taken that biblical principle, removed love from it, and forbidden dancing in their congregations because they *know* dancing leads to all sorts of despicable sins. So now, generations of people with good hearts cannot use dance to express their love for God (as David did) or their spouse because they are bound by religion.

Please do not misunderstand me: we must follow God's commands. However, if we apply the characteristics of agape love, we see that the love of God "thinks no evil" (1 Cor. 13:5).

Why do we make up rules based on what people *might* do? The reason is because we do not filter our good intentions through the SMS of God's love. God loved us so much that He gave us the ultimate example of His love, which is Jesus. Jesus set us free, and if the Son makes us free, then we are free indeed (see John 8:36).

Colossians 2:20-23 says, "Therefore, if you died with Christ from the basic principles of the world, why, as though living in the world, do you subject yourselves to regulations—'Do not touch, do not taste, do not handle,' which all concern things which perish with the using—according to the commandments and doctrines of men? These things indeed have an appearance of wisdom in self-imposed religion, false humility, and neglect of the body, but are of no value against the indulgence of the flesh."

The weapon of the Word filtered through love tells us that we are free. Again, please do not misunderstand me—just because we are free does not mean that we have a license to sin. We can be free and still do what is right by taking God's commandments, filtering them through love, and asking Him, "Would You be pleased if I did this (whatever 'this' may be)?" When handling the Word this way, it becomes a liberating spiritual force that will conquer anything that dares oppose it.

Galatians 5:6 tells us, "In Christ Jesus neither circumcision nor uncircumcision avails anything, but *faith working through love*" (emphasis added). First Corinthians 13:2-3 says, "And though I have the gift of prophecy, and understand all mysteries and all knowledge, *and though I have all faith, so that I could remove mountains, but have not love, I am nothing.* And though I bestow all my goods to feed the poor, and though I give my body to be burned, but have not love, it profits me nothing" (emphasis added). When the weapon of faith is not controlled by love, it is useless. Everything that God does is done through faith.

Since we were created in His image, we, too, must operate on the principles of faith. Everything that we create must be by faith. The outcomes of our creations are determined by how they are created. If they are created by faith, working by love, they will bring us closer to God. However, apart from the love of God, those creations will move us further from God, because they will be done out of our own selfish desires.

To illustrate this idea, think about the entertainment industry. It took tremendous faith for people to build our modern entertainment industry. However, most of the movies, games and television shows that are released today relay messages that are contrary to the love of God. First John 2:15-16 says, "Do not love the world or the things in the world. If anyone loves the world, the love of the Father is not in him. For all that is in the world—the lust of the flesh, the lust of the eyes, and the pride of life—is not of the Father but is of the world." The majority of the entertainment industry is built on these ideas, which take us further from God because He is not in them.

However, entertainment created with a love of God mentality is much different. Now, I know everything is not perfect in today's Christian entertainment, but the majority of the media that the Christian entertainment industry releases is for the purpose of moving people closer to God. Most Christian songwriters have the faith that they have heard a message from God, which they then want to relay to those who will listen. Such musicians truly believe that God has given them the talent to put notes together in a way that is pleasing to the listener so that he or she can hear the message of the song. It is the system of love for God and love of people that uses the talents God has given to help spread the gospel to as many different people as possible. *Do* the entertainers benefit from it? Sure they do. However, most will take any profit or fame they receive to further advance the kingdom of God.

The world's financial system is built on the same principles as the world's entertainment system. "Get what you can while you can." "The man with the most toys wins." "Why pass up this once in a lifetime opportunity?" "Pay no interest for three years." All of these are slogans that appeal to the "self" mentality. By falling for these schemes, the Christian Church has found itself broke, in debt, and unable to fund the spreading of the gospel as God has intended. God's financial system is totally opposite to the world's system. Luke 6:38 says, "Give, and it will be given to you: good measure, pressed down, shaken together, and running over will be put into your bosom. For with the same measure that you use, it will be measured back to you." God's financial system is built on giving, because it is built on love and love gives.

There is a clear reason why faith, when used with the love of God, will create opportunities that bring us closer to Him. Romans 10:17 says, "Faith comes by hearing and hearing by the word of God." God is love, so His Word is full of love. We obtain faith when we realize that His Word is His Son. When we are purposeful about hearing God's Word, we allow Jesus to become more real to us. Knowing that His Son has conquered Satan and this world system then gives us the faith to overcome anything in our lives and allows us to use His power to set others free. That is why faith, when filtered through love, gives us the ability to create situations that will bring people closer to God, thereby enabling us to realize His goodness.

As we mentioned in the last chapter, prayer is the tool by which our recreated spirits communicate with the Father. Because God is love and everything that comes from Him is full of love, prayer becomes the love language in our relationship with Him. First Corinthians 13:4-8 lets us know how our lives should reflect God's love: "Love suffers long and is kind; love does not envy; love does not parade itself, is not puffed up; does not behave rudely, does not seek its own, is not provoked, thinks no evil; does not rejoice in iniquity, but rejoices in the truth; bears all things, believes all things, hopes all things, endures all things. Love never fails."

Even though prayer is a mighty weapon, if it is not filtered by love, it becomes self-seeking. How many times have we started praying for someone only to change direction and begin praying for ourselves? James 4:3 says, "You ask and do not receive because you ask amiss, that you may spend it on your pleasures." Remember, love elevates the person loved to the highest position that he or she can go, which is at the Father's feet.

If we are walking in love toward God, our desire will be to spend time with Him and communicate with Him. We should desire to express our gratitude for what He has done and what He is doing as well as for what He will do. We should also communicate our love to Jesus by acknowledging His Lordship and giving Him thanks for the sacrifice He made. We need to thank Him for continually interceding for us and let Him know that we cannot wait for His return. Love should motivate us to communicate with the Holy Spirit and thank Him for His instruction, comfort, and display of power in our lives.

If we are going to walk in love, we will not stop at loving God. If we love God, we will love what He loves. God loves the world, and if He loves it, we must love it as well. We must make a decision that no matter what the world does to us, we will love it and all the people in it. This is only possible when we are able to fully grasp the love that God displayed when He sent His Son to die for our sins. Knowing the price that God paid to set us free should drive us to be whole and without need.

Jesus humbled Himself when he left the throne of God in heaven and came to suffer and die for us. He provided everything we need to make us complete. Colossians 2:10 says, "You are complete in Him, who is the head of all principality and power." James 1:4 says, "But let patience have its perfect work, that you may be perfect and complete, lacking nothing." Acknowledging that God loved us enough to give us "everything that pertains to life and godliness" (2 Pet. 1:3) through the sacrifice of His Son will make us whole and without need. Once we have established the fact that we are whole in Christ Jesus, we are in a better position to do what God commanded, which is to love our neighbor. Without love for our neighbor, we will not care if their needs are met or even if they go to hell.

"We love Him because He first loved us" (1 John 4:19). It is God's love that motivates us to do what He has commanded. It is His love that drives us to His Word, keeps us in our prayer closet and gives us the ability to sacrificially share with our neighbors. God has given us spiritual weapons so that we can live victoriously in this life. However, if we do not employ these weapons through love, the precision of each weapon will be diminished and our effectiveness will be minimized.

CHAPTER 8

Mutual Support

THE POTENTIAL FIREPOWER of the F-16 is tremendous. However, it would be hard to find an F-16 pilot that would go into combat alone. All fighter pilots have studied the principles of warfare, and one of these principles is to never be caught alone. When pilots are alone, they become easy prey for the enemy.

Most fighter missions are flown with a minimum of two aircraft that work together as a team. In the Air Force, this team is called an "element" or a "flight." In the Navy or Marines, it is called a "section." The element or section is the basic fighting unit of a fighter squadron. These units make up larger groups, but the primary reason there is a minimum of two is to ensure that mutual support can be maintained.

The element is normally made up of a flight lead and a wingman. The flight lead is a pilot who has obtained his or her position by experience and a demonstration of leadership skills. The wingman is normally not as experienced as the flight lead and is put in the position of wingman to support his or her flight lead. The leader and wingman have defined duties to execute during any mission. The flight lead is responsible for the overall conduct of the flight, for navigation to the target and for how weapons are to be employed. The wingman's primary responsibilities are to be a visual lookout and to back up the flight lead.

The main reason mutual support is so important is because of the physical limitations of both the aircraft and the pilot. One of the aircraft's limitations is the inability of its radar to look at the entire airspace around it. Fighter aircraft are relatively small; therefore, they cannot carry a large radar antenna required to view large areas. As a result of theses physical limitations, the pilot of a fighter is unable to look for enemy aircraft from the surface to 45,000 feet (see figure 3). However, two fighters can watch the entire area by having one fighter look from the surface up to 25,000 feet and the other fighter look from 20,000 feet up to 45,000 feet.

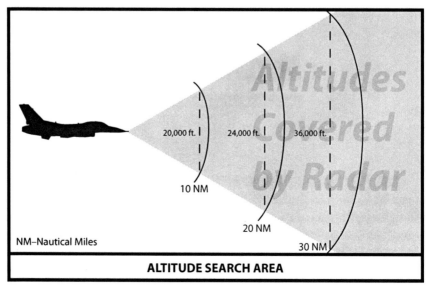

Figure 3

One of the physical limitation of an F-16 pilot is the inability to turn his or her head completely around in the cockpit, which is what he or she would have to do to see an enemy aircraft coming directly behind the aircraft. However, with two aircraft visual lookout becomes much easier, because each pilot can check behind ("checking six") the other aircraft. Figure 4 shows how two aircraft make it easier to see behind each other. With one to two miles of separation between the two aircraft, it is very easy for the pilots to ensure that an enemy aircraft will not able to slip into the lethality zone of the wingman's aircraft (within two miles) without being detected.

On any mission, there are numerous duties that must be accomplished if a mission is to be successful. A plan has to be developed, navigation to the target must be accomplished, threats must be negated, targets must be destroyed, and then the flight has to get home. The continual flow of information that must be processed to accomplish those tasks is too much for one person to handle. Working as a team divides the various tasks so one person is not overloaded, and fewer mistakes are made.

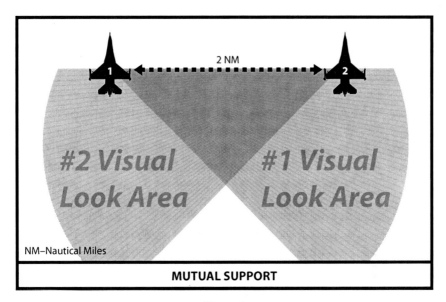

MUTUAL SUPPORT

Figure 4

Mutual support not only helps to negate some aircraft and pilot limitations but also aids in the effectual delivery of various weapons. When an element is attacking a target, one fighter (called the "engaged fighter") actively delivers the weapons while a supporting fighter watches for enemies that could become a threat to the engaged fighter. This process allows the engaged fighter pilot to concentrate on the delivery of his or her weapons without being concerned with other distractions. When operating properly, the flight lead/wingman relationship is a wonderful display of teamwork and coordination.

Mutual support in our Christian lives is as important as mutual support in the fighter community. We live in a hostile environment. If we are to be successful in the presentation of the gospel, which is our mission, we must maintain mutual support. Our mission is much too hard for each of us to handle alone. We all have spiritual limitations, and there is not one Christian who has all of the spiritual gifts operating in his or her life to its fullness. We have all the gifts available to use when we need them, but there are certain individuals who have a special anointing for healing, for faith, for prophecy and so forth. In addition, spiritual plans have to be developed, navigation along the path of those plans has to be accomplished, resistance to the enemy must be maintained, and the message of the gospel must be delivered. This is why God always puts us with a group of believers.

Ecclesiastes 4:9-12 says, "Two are better than one, because they have a good reward for their labor. For if they fall, one will lift up his companion. But woe to him who is alone when he falls, for he has no one to help him up. Again, if two lie down together, they will keep warm; but how can one be warm alone? Though one may be overpowered by another, two can withstand him. And a threefold cord is not quickly broken." God is aware of the fact that we need help in our spiritual battles. In Genesis 2:18, He says, "It is not good that man should be alone." Too often, though, we are deceived into thinking that we can minister on our own and end up as easy prey for the enemy. If everyone is involved in ministering, problems will arise because a "watchman" is not looking out for the tactics that Satan will try to use to stop what is happening. To be effective, one person has to be engaged in ministering while another watches for spiritual threats. This is God's design to prevent one person from being over tasked and making mistakes as a result.

Mutual support can break down in several different ways. The first way it breaks down is through inattention to the task at hand. For instance, a flight lead may call a turn that the wingman does not hear. When the lead turns, the wingman does not follow, and the two are separated. Mutual support will also not work if the defined roles are not maintained. A leader that does not delegate to his or her wingman will quickly be over-tasked, which will ultimately lead to mistakes. Likewise, a wingman that tries to take over the leader's duties will not be able to support the flight lead and will allow a crack for the enemy to enter.

In Luke 10, when Jesus sent out the Seventy, He sent them out two by two. When Paul went on his missionary journeys, he always took someone with him. If Jesus and Paul knew the importance of mutual support, we should also adhere to the biblical principle of not performing ministry by ourselves. We need to learn how to operate as teams in order to maximize our effectiveness in enemy territory.

It is never a good idea to minister alone just like it is not good to go into battle alone. However, there will be times when ministry must be done alone due to the situation at hand. When those situations occur, realize that Jesus and the Holy Spirit will be there to assist and protect you. This will be the exception rather than the rule, but do not pass up a ministry opportunity just because there is no one to assist. Pray, and know that if God tells you to continue, He will back you up.

Mutual support is vitally important in the "Fighter" community and it must be adhered to in the "Christian" community as well. God knows our limitations and has provided others to make up for our deficiencies. We can never have a "one man" mentality and survive against our knowledgeable and strong enemy. To accomplish our mission of spreading the Gospel of Jesus Christ, we must employ the strengths God has given each of us in coordinated efforts. Working together, we can successfully navigate to our target, defeat the threats along the way and defeat our enemy as we storm the gates of Hell to rescue those held in bondage to the devil.

CHAPTER 9

TACTICS OF THE ENEMY

THE MOVIE *PATTON* is one of my favorite classic World War II movies. In one scene, General Patton (played by George C. Scott) is on a high plateau watching a battle between his forces and General Rommel's German forces. As the conflict between the opposing tanks draws to a close, Patton, realizing his forces have won, excitingly exclaims, "Rommel [some words deleted], I read your book!" Even though the German tanks were superior, Patton had studied Rommel's tactics and had designed his tactics to effectively defeat the Germans.

Second Corinthians 10:3 tells us, "For though we walk in the flesh, we do not war according to the flesh." Ephesians 6:12 says, "For we do not wrestle against flesh and blood but against principalities, against powers, against the rulers of the darkness of this age, against spiritual hosts of wickedness in the heavenly places." As Christians, we must understand that we are at war. However, it is imperative that we also know whom we are fighting against and the tactics our enemy employs.

One of the biggest frustrations of the soldiers in the Vietnam War was that it was difficult for them to identify whom they were fighting. Before a warrior can effectively fight an adversary, he or she must know exactly who it is that he or she is warring against. Once the enemy is identified, the warrior must then determine how the enemy operates so he or she can effectively use the weapons that have been given to them. In this chapter, we will identify our spiritual enemy and discuss the tactics he uses. Before I get into those ideas, however, I believe it is important to first look at the way an adversary will attempt to defeat his enemy. That information will then be applied to our spiritual enemy.

Normally, when a country determines it wants to conquer another country, it will not employ its military first. Instead, it will attempt to influence the decisions of the other country's people through a propaganda campaign. The reason the attacking country attempts this tactic is to see if it can win a cheap victory. If it can achieve its objectives without committing any troops, it can save its resources for other battles.

The main tactic used in any propaganda campaign is division. The attacking country will use one faction against another, promote the side that is in agreement with its agenda, and criticize the side that does not agree with it. The primary goal of the attacking country during the propaganda campaign is to defeat its adversary from within. As long as this destruction is going in the direction the attacking country wants, it will not have to commit precious resources and will win a quick and easy victory. However, if the attacking country sees the propaganda campaign failing, it will then be forced to commit troops in an attempt to impose its will on the people it is attacking.

There are different levels of troop commitment. The first level will be an attempt to win battles through deception using small numbers of troops. If that tactic does not achieve the desired objective, the attacking country will be forced to overwhelm their enemy.

When a country threatens another country, there are several criteria that can be used to judge the creditability of an enemy's threat. One of the main items to evaluate is the number of warriors in the enemy's army. For example, a threat of invasion from Libya would not be taken as seriously as a threat of invasion from China due to the difference in the size of their armies. After looking at the numbers, the next item to evaluate is the enemy's equipment and its capability to employ that equipment. Iraq was considered a significant threat before the first Gulf War not because of its massive manpower but because of the tremendous number of tanks, aircraft, and other weapons it possessed.

Once the enemy has been identified and verified as a legitimate threat, the way it operates must be broken down. Every military uses the weapons available to it in specific ways. These mannerisms are called tactics. To be consistently successful against an enemy, soldiers must know the tactics their enemy uses. This knowledge allows them to predict what they will encounter on the battlefield and then effectively counter those tactics to gain an advantage over the enemy. Without knowledge of the adversary's tactics or common tendencies, soldiers are forced into a reactive mode, which gives an advantage to their opponent. The quality of the soldiers' adversary is determined by the complexity of its tactics, which will then determine the level of training the soldiers need to counter those tactics.

Since the 1950s, Russia (the former Soviet Union) has been considered the primary enemy of the United States. The arms race, the proliferation of nuclear weapons, and the Cold War are identifiable evidences of that fact. All of the wars the United States has been involved in since World War II have been against enemies trained by the Russians using mostly Russian equipment. As a result, our military has trained extensively against Russian tactics. Because I am not an expert on Russian navel or army tactics, I can only authoritatively discuss the area I am very acquainted with: their Air Force. The Russian Air Force is a very formidable adversary. It has a large number of very good aircraft that can carry excellent weapons. When I was flying F-16s, the MIG-29 Fulcrum and the SU-27 Flanker were the two best aircraft that they possessed. These are extremely maneuverable aircraft that are comparable to our best fighters—the F-14, F-15, F-16, and F-18. The weapons they can carry, if measured by performance alone, are actually better than ours. In fact, if air superiority were based solely on equipment and weapons, the Russians would have a distinct advantage.

Fortunately for us, there are other elements that go into determining who possesses the best fighting machine. The avionics systems (radar, weapon control system, navigation systems) in our aircraft are much more sophisticated, giving our pilots a better picture of what is going on around them. In addition, our communication processes and command and control structure are far better than the Russian's. Our superiority also lies in the ability of our pilots to improvise when the tactics they employ do not work exactly the way they were drawn up on the board. American pilots are trained to be disciplined but also creative in combat situations. They are allowed to think for themselves as long as they stay within the confines of the rules of engagement.

Now that we have determined the Russian Air Force to be a credible threat, we must next define the tactics it employs. Russian air tactics are very effective, but a main weakness lies in the inability of its pilots to improvise. Although their pilots are improving, they still are very rigid in the way they fly and do not show much creativity. The reason they are so rigid is because they are dependent on a central control agency. Due to this rigidity, their pilots are very predictable, which makes them easier to defeat. If American pilots learn how and why the Russian pilots use the tactics they employ and then learn how to counter them, they can be very successful against them.

In my combat squadrons, we spent hours reading manuals about Russian tactics. We studied the tactics they employ and how to defeat each one. We used the lessons we learned in this benign classroom environment in our training sorties. Almost all of our training sorties were flown against our own aircraft simulating Russian tactics. This training method equipped us to quickly recognize what we were up against and then counter whatever tactic we saw.

The flying portion of the training was essential because lessons are easy to understand while sitting in a comfortable classroom or reading a tactics manual (we affectionately call this the "1G environment"), but they can be hard to put into practice in real life. The real test of the fighter pilots' comprehension came during the training flights. If they could react properly to the information they saw on their radar or heard from outside sources while traveling at more than 500 mph and feeling the effects of the G-forces, then it could be ascertained that the pilots understood what they had been taught.

There are two primary tactics employed by Russian pilots or pilots trained by the Russians: deception and overwhelming with numbers. Deception is the preferred tactic, because it accomplishes the destruction of an opponent's aircraft without committing a large number of their aircraft. However, if deception does not serve their objective, those in command will not hesitate to attempt to overwhelm their opponent with a lot of aircraft.

The primary goal of the Russian's deception tactics is to enable one or more of their aircraft to reach the aircraft they are attacking without their adversary detecting they are there. If they achieve this objective, they possess a tremendous advantage at the point the weapons begin to be exchanged (we call this "the merge"). As our Air Force studied their deception tactics, we gave names such as "stack," "post hole," "resolution cell" and "lead around" to each one. We used these names as a means of effectively communicating the formations of the attacking aircraft to our fellow fighter pilots.

In any of our air-to-air situations, there were three things we had to determine to achieve a successful outcome: (1) how many aircraft we were going against, (2) what formation the enemy was flying (the name of the formation), and (3) what the enemy was doing in the formation. To explain this better, I will explain how we would attack the "stack" formation (see figure 5).

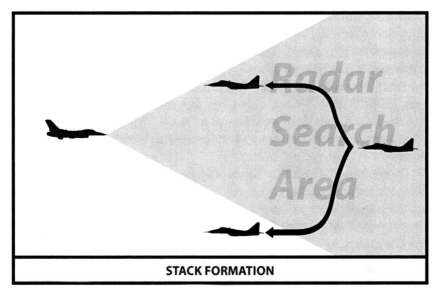

STACK FORMATION

Figure 5

The "stack" was a formation of two or more groups of aircraft on top of each other with at least 10,000 feet of altitude separation. The purpose of this tactic was to see if either the high or low group of aircraft could be targeted without detecting the other group at the different altitude. If only one group was targeted, the other group of aircraft was free to engage their adversary without them knowing they were there (a very unhealthy situation to be in). To counter this tactic, we had to maintain a disciplined radar search pattern (look with our aircraft's radar).

As I mentioned, the F-16's radar is limited because of the size of the receivers and transmitters that can be put on a fighter-sized aircraft. It therefore cannot detect targets in all parts of the sky. To counteract this, we assigned each aircraft in our formation specific altitude blocks and azimuth scans (certain number of degrees to the left and right of the aircraft's nose) to ensure that every possible area was covered. As I stated previously, we normally flew in groups of two or more—a flight lead and a wingman. The flight lead would determine where to search with his or her radar, while the wingmen would search in another designated area. For example, if I was leading a two-ship (two F 16s) and I believed the highest potential threat would come from above us, I would search with my radar from an altitude of 45,000 feet down to as far as my radar could go. My wingman would then search from the ground level up to as far as his radar could go.

So, if the enemy came at us in a stack, I would identify what I saw on my radar by saying, "Bandit, nose [which means in front of us] thirty-five miles at three nine zero [39,000 feet]." This would tell my wingman what I believed we were up against. My wingman would answer by telling me what he saw on his radar: "Bandit nose, thirty-five miles at one nine zero [19,000 feet]." Recognizing the different altitudes, my wingman or I would call out the formation as a "stack." We had now identified what formation our enemy was employing and how many aircraft were present.

It was important for us to identify the formation so that we could determine the most advantageous way to counter it. In this case, we would stay together as long as possible and then split our formation. One of us would go after the high group while the other would go after the low group. As a general rule, we tried not to split our forces because there were tremendous advantages in staying together for as long as possible. However, if we were forced to split, as was necessary against the stack formation, we would have a plan for our forces to rejoin as soon as possible.

The stack was just one type of deception tactic. There were variations of the stack as well as the other deception tactics. If we were able to successfully defeat our enemy's deception tactics (or the variations of it) in a battle situation, we could expect them to employ the next level of tactics and attempt to overwhelm us. This next level required a higher commitment of forces from our enemy, so we knew that they would come at us in more numerous groups.

One of the Russian's overwhelming tactics was called a "champagne"(see figure 6). This tactic involved several groups of aircraft coming at us at different altitudes and different positions relative to our aircraft's nose. Normally, this formation would start as a single group and then split into different groups at a predetermined range from our aircraft. One group would go left, one group would go right, and one group would continue at us from the middle. If someone were to look at this formation from above (which we called "the God's eye view"), it would look like a champagne glass.

There were a couple of important points for us to remember when we went against overwhelming tactics such as the champagne. The first was that we could not fight against this tactic alone. We had to have the support of a wingman and additional outside help to be successful. This outside help was either a land based radar controller or a controller aboard an AWACS (Airborne Warning and Control System) aircraft. The second

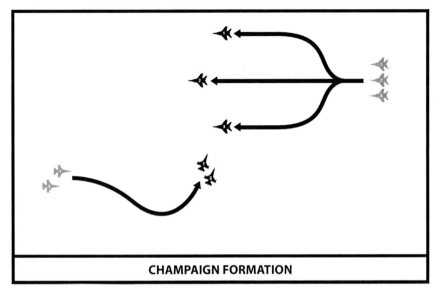

CHAMPAIGN FORMATION

Figure 6

point was that we could not spend a lot of time in trying to defeat one group. If we spent too much time on one group, the other groups would have time to get close enough to employ weapons against us (once again a very dangerous position to be in).

One aspect common to both deception tactics and overwhelming tactics was that the timing of each had to be correct in order for it to work. The goal of each of these tactics was to change something while the adversary was busy doing something else or to time compress the enemy making it virtually impossible to manage everything that was happening. If the tactic was executed too far away from our aircraft, we had enough time to sort everyone out before the shooting started. If the tactic was performed too close to our aircraft, the deception would not have sufficient time to develop causing the groups to be too close together which would not cause the overwhelming or deception situation desired.

The training we received made us very proficient at recognizing these deception and overwhelming tactics. If we were able to recognize our adversary's formation and execute the proper response, we were rarely defeated.

By now, you might be asking why I'm telling you all of this. The reason is because the tactics used by our enemy in spiritual warfare are very similar to the tactics used by the Russians. Scripture is clear about who our spiritual enemy is. First Peter 5:8 tells us, "Be sober be vigilant; because your adversary *the devil* walks about like a roaring lion, seeking whom he may devour" (emphasis added). First John 3:8 tells us, "For this purpose the Son of God was manifested, that He might destroy the works of the devil." From the Garden of Eden in Genesis to the defeat of the devil in Revelation, our enemy is identified, and his name is Satan.

Satan is a spiritual being, so we must do battle with him in the spiritual realm using spiritual weapons. The Word of God is our tactics manual to study our adversary's tactics. The time we spend at church is our classroom time to learn how others have defeated the enemy and to build camaraderie between fellow warriors so that we can effectively come against our enemy (this is one of the reasons why church attendance is so important). As Christians, we must understand what authority Jesus has given us in order to fully enjoy the position of superiority over our adversary, the devil. First Peter 5:8 reveals to us that the devil has to look for someone to destroy. The devil cannot destroy someone who has authority over him (authority given by Jesus Christ) unless that person allows the devil to destroy him or her.

Our enemy, Satan, is a very creditable threat. He has a large army of well-trained warriors equipped with weapons such as lust, fear, doubt, deception, anger, hate, and pride. These are time-tested weapons that are powerful and effective on anyone who is not prepared to resist them. Examples of Satan's power can be seen in Exodus when the magicians in Pharaoh's court imitated what God did when He turned Aaron's rod into a snake. Modern examples of Satan's power include a dad abusing his kids, a person taking another's life for no apparent reason, or an individual completely destroying his or her life with drugs.

Just as with a propaganda campaign, the devil will first try to get us to defeat ourselves before he uses his forces. If that does not work, he will commit his forces to deceive us. If his deception tactics are not successful, he will then try to overwhelm us with numbers. We must learn the tactics of our enemy so that we do not fall prey to his destructive work. When we do not understand what tactics the devil uses, we subject ourselves to all sorts of evil. We are put in a reactive mode and are unable to identify and effectively counter the tactics being employed against us.

The devil will never stop trying to defeat God by defeating us. However, this should not give us cause to fear, because Jesus Christ has already defeated Satan and all his demons. Furthermore, we need to remember two important facts that will instill confidence in our ability (through Jesus) to defeat the devil. First, most scholars agree that when Satan fell, one-third of the angels fell with him. If *one-third* fell, it means *two-thirds* remained, which means the bad angels are outnumbered by the good angels two to one. Second, unlike humans, Satan was *not* created in the image of God. He was created with specific capabilities and talents, but he does not possess a creative ability such as God gave to man. By understanding this fact, we can ascertain that just as the Russians are very predictable, the devil is also very predictable, as he does not have the ability to create new ways of doing things. We can also ascertain that the demons under the devil's authority cannot do anything apart from what they are told, as they are followers under a higher authority. They are controlled by a central power and must obey the higher authority.

Since the devil does not have creative ability, he is using the same tactics today as he did when he first deceived Eve in the Garden of Eden. Scripture can be our tactics manual that describes exactly how Satan operates. Look at Genesis 3:1-6:

> Now the serpent was more cunning than any beast of the field which the LORD God had made. And he said to the woman, "Has God indeed said, 'You shall not eat of every tree of the garden?'" And the woman said to the serpent, 'We may eat the fruit of the trees of the garden; but of the fruit of the tree which is in the midst of the garden, God has said, "You shall not eat it, nor shall you touch it, lest you die."' Then the serpent said to the woman, 'You will not surely die. For God knows that in the day you eat of it your eyes will be opened, and you will be like God, knowing good and evil.' So when the woman saw that the tree was good for food, that it was pleasant to the eyes, and a tree desirable to make one wise, she took of its fruit and ate. She also gave to her husband with her, and he ate.

How did Satan tempt Eve? He tempted her by appealing to her hunger ("the woman saw the tree was good for food"), to her eyes ("it was pleasant to the eyes"), and to her desire to be wise ("a tree desirable to make one wise"). Now look at how Satan tempted Jesus in Matthew 4:1-11:

> Then Jesus was led up by the Spirit into the wilderness to be tempted by the devil. And when He had fasted forty days and forty nights, afterward He was hungry. Now when the tempter came to Him, he said, "If You

are the Son of God, command that these stones become bread." But
He answered and said, "It is written, Man shall not live by bread alone,
but by every word that proceeds from the mouth of God." Then the
devil took Him up into the holy city, set Him on the pinnacle of the
temple, and said to Him, "If You are the Son of God, throw Yourself
down. For it is written: 'He shall give His angels charge over you, and,
in their hands they shall bear you up, lest you dash your foot against
a stone.'" Jesus said to him, "It is written again, 'You shall not tempt
the Lord your God.'" Again, the devil took Him up on an exceedingly
high mountain, and showed Him all the kingdoms of the world and
their glory. And he said to Him, "All these things I will give You if You
will fall down and worship me." Then Jesus said to him, "Away with
you, Satan! For it is written, 'You shall worship the Lord your God, and
Him only you shall serve.'" Then the devil left Him, and behold, angels
came and ministered to Him.

The devil first tempted Jesus by appealing to His appetite, then by
appealing to His position, and finally by showing Jesus all the kingdoms
of the world (I'll bet they were beautiful too!). First John 2:15-16 says,
"Do not love the world or the things in the world. If anyone loves the
world, the love of the Father is not in him. For *all* that is in the world—the
lust of the flesh, the lust of the eyes, and the pride of life—is not of the
Father but is of the world." Satan still uses the lust of the flesh as he did
with Eve and Jesus when he appealed to their appetites. He still uses
the lust of the eyes as he did with Eve (she saw the fruit of the tree was
pleasant to the eyes) and with Jesus (all the kingdoms of the world had
to be beautiful). He also uses the boastful pride of life just as he did with
Eve (he told her she could be just as wise as God) and Jesus (he tried to
appeal to His special status as God's Son by telling Him He could throw
Himself off the Temple and God would protect Him).

Look at the first part of 1 John 2:16 again: "For *all* that is in the
world—the lust of the flesh, the lust of the eyes, and the pride of life"
(emphasis added). All that Satan has to work with are various forms
of these three tactics. Knowing this should put us in an advantageous
position. Once we read our tactics manual, the Bible, and determine how
to recognize Satan's tactics, we are empowered to walk in total victory
as long as we maintain our focus and follow God's plan.

As I mentioned, in any type of confrontation, a country would prefer
to defeat its opponent without ever having to commit troops or equipment
to do so. Satan is not any different. If he can get Christians lulled into

complacency or into a state of unwillingness to fight, he has won the war without ever having to commit his troops. For example, if a church is beginning to do mighty things for the kingdom of God, Satan might try to create an internal division over some minor point in Scripture or over how a certain matter should be handled. Satan hasn't committed any spiritual forces; he has just tempted the congregants to fight among themselves. If they do not recognize Satan as the source of this division and properly deal with it, they may begin attacking each other and hand Satan an easy victory. The reason Satan wins in such a situation is because the Holy Spirit is not free to work in an atmosphere of division or strife. When the Holy Spirit is not free to move, the effective work of God comes to a standstill.

If we are able to recognize and fight these temptations properly, it won't be long before Satan will begin committing his spiritual hosts of wickedness to stop the spread of the gospel.

Once Satan begins to directly attack us, those attacks will most likely be in the form of various types of deception. He will bring different weapons against us in an effort to divert our attention so that he can sneak up and destroy us.

Let me explain it this way. Recently, a church I was attending began to see a move of God. People were getting saved and manifestations of healings were taking place. There was one man who had endured severe pain in his head for twenty-three years. The doctors had told him there was nothing they could do for him. Members of the church prayed for him, and one week later the pain had totally vanished. He was miraculously healed. Praise God!

At that point, Satan could not stand it any longer. Two days after we received the report of the man's healing, a woman who had sought help from our church committed suicide. Which of the two events received more attention? To our shame, the suicide got most of the attention. Most of our attention and energy was directed at dealing with the very visible problem of the suicide. The pastor preached sermons, and the Sunday School leaders devoted time to deal with this problem. At the same time, groups of people began to unjustly blame other groups for the death of the woman. All the attention was devoted to the visible enemy, which was the spirit of suicide, and nothing was done about the strife and division that was attacking at the same time. We fell for one of Satan's deception tactics. We paid too much attention to the highly visible enemy and ignored the enemies coming at us from treetop level. The move of God was stopped until we dealt with the strife and division.

When something visible comes against us, we must be aware that, most likely, something else is out there. We must maintain a disciplined radar search through the Holy Spirit to identify *all* of our enemies. That is why intercessory prayer is vital in a church. Through prayer, God can reveal the tactics the enemy is using. Intercessory prayer is our intelligence service that spies on our enemy and tells us his next move. Prayer allows the Holy Spirit to be our radar so that we can see the less visible enemies. Unless we deal with the enemies coming at treetop level, we will never be in a strategically advantageous position to defeat the more visible threats.

Deception tactics come in many different forms, but the goal is always to divert attention from one group so that another group can come into the fight undetected and steal, kill and destroy. To properly counter deception tactics, we must be diligent to maintain our mutual support, as well as praying and keeping a constant lookout for things that are not obvious. By doing these things, we can prevent Satan from winning a battle through deception.

If Satan's initial tactics fail, he may use another maneuver such as the Russian champagne tactic. Maybe everything in our lives is going fine when all of a sudden a very appealing business deal comes up that has the capability of making us a lot of money. At the same time, we experience a physical problem that makes us wonder if there is something seriously wrong with our health. If that were not enough, we also begin to have increased demands on our time from family, friends and church. What has Satan done? He has committed different forces at different places to hopefully get us attacking one group of problems while disregarding (or not even seeing) another group that can defeat us. In this situation, the only way to effectively defeat the devil is to be prepared. The only victors in this type of battle will be those who have taken the time to study and meditate on God's Word, those who have kept the lines of communication open between their Commander and themselves, and those who have allowed the Holy Spirit to be their radar.

Look at Mark 4:13-20. In this passage, Jesus explains the tactics Satan uses. When we hear the good news of the gospel, Satan immediately comes in to steal that word (see v. 15). If that does not work, he will deploy forces to defeat us through tribulation and persecution (see v. 17). This is where our awareness of deceptive tactics comes into play. If we remain vigilant and fight Satan's attacks, he will be required to devote more resources to try and distract us from the truth of the Word. He does this by presenting multiple fronts to get us off of the course that God has for us. The Bible describes these as "the cares of this world [bills, marriage, friendship and such], the deceitfulness of riches, and the desire for other things" (v. 19). The good news is that if we continue to follow God and remain steadfast in the Word, we will produce fruit in our lives.

Our example of victorious living is Jesus Christ. He was fully man, just as we are. He was tempted, just as we are (see Heb. 4:14-15). However, He never sinned. He was always ready for the spiritual battles He encountered. Because of what Jesus did, we too can be prepared for every battle that we will go through. First Corinthians 10:13 says, "No temptation has overtaken you except such as is common to man; but God is faithful, who will not allow you to be tempted beyond what you are able, but with the temptation will also make the way of escape, that you may be able to bear it." God's grace and mercy will not allow us to go through anything for which we are not prepared.

There is no excuse for failure. God has prearranged the victorious status we have through the sacrifice of His Son, Jesus. Jesus gave us every weapon necessary to effectively defeat Satan and his forces. As we pray, God, through the Holy Spirit, will enable us to recognize Satan's tactics for what they are. As we read and meditate on His Word, our faith will increase to the point we can quench every fiery dart of our enemy (see Eph. 6:16). The Word of God also will give us the confidence to continue our warfare against Satan.

Paul experienced the "overwhelming" tactic during his ministry. Everywhere he turned, his efforts to spread the gospel were thwarted. In 2 Corinthians 11:23, Paul explained how Satan tried everything in his power to stop the spread of the gospel:

> Are they ministers of Christ?—I speak as a fool—I am more: in labors more abundant, in stripes above measure, in prisons more frequently, in deaths often. From the Jews five times I received forty stripes minus one. Three times I was beaten with rods; once I was stoned; three times I was shipwrecked; a night and a day I have been in the deep; in journeys often, in perils of waters, in perils of robbers, in perils of my own countrymen, in perils of the Gentiles, in perils in the city, in perils in the wilderness, in perils in the sea, in perils among false brethren, in weariness and toil, in sleeplessness often, in hunger and thirst, in fastings often, in cold and nakedness—besides the other things, what comes upon me daily: my deep concern for all the churches.

Satan threw everything he had at Paul. However, Paul was able to exclaim in Romans 8:37, "Yet in all these things we are more than conquerors through Him who loved us." Paul understood that the weapons he had been given were sufficient to defeat any attack the devil made against him. He understood that as long as he remained in Christ, nothing in this world could defeat him. John also understood this concept. He wrote in 1 John 5:4-5, "For whatever is born of God overcomes the world. And this is the victory that has overcome the world—our faith. Who is he who overcomes the world, but he who believes that Jesus is the Son of God?"

Everything we need to walk victoriously has been given to us. God will commit everything in heaven to ensure our victory. We must have confidence that God's army is bigger than the devil's and that our spiritual weapons are mightier than his. Developing our faith through prayer and reading God's Word will give us confidence in our superiority over the devil's tactics and put us in a position to see Satan defeated before our very eyes. When this occurs, we will exclaim, "Satan, you lying thief, I beat you because I read the Book!"

CHAPTER 10

A DECLARATION OF WAR

FEW PEOPLE DESIRE war. Most prefer to try negotiations or sanctions to solve the problem between nations that are at odds with one another. Sometimes, negotiations and sanctions do work, but at other times there is no recourse but to declare war.

The United States is very cautious about entering a war. This country has determined that it will only commit forces to a war in situations where our national security or the security of one of our allies is being threatened. That is what happened in the first Gulf War. Kuwait and Saudi Arabia were considered allies of the United States. Since we import much of our oil from Saudi Arabia, we could not sit back and allow a dictator like Saddam Hussein to take over those countries. The result would have been destabilization in the region and an unstable dictator controlling a large portion of the world's oil supply. Iraq had already invaded Kuwait, and Saddam was using that small country as a staging ground to threaten Saudi Arabia. When diplomacy failed and it appeared that Iraq would attack Saudi Arabia, the United States had to declare war against Iraq to stop Saddam Hussein.

Spiritual wars are no different. There is an aggressor, whose name is Satan, and he and his army have declared war on God's most precious creation, which is humankind. Negotiations to stop his aggression have failed. When we accept Jesus Christ as our Savior, we become a tremendous threat to Satan's kingdom. Satan hates anything that God loves—especially His children. He wants to invade our homeland so that he can steal all we have, kill everything precious to us, and destroy everything we have ever done (see John 10:10).

Satan knows that he does not have any spiritual authority to do anything to a Christian because we are part of God's family. However, he is aware that if he can find a place where a Christian will not fight against him then he legally has a way to attack. Satan will use our natural aversion for war against us. Like any aggressor, he will try to get the people he is attempting to conquer in a position where they do not have the heart to fight. All aggressors know that if they can remove a people's will to fight, the victory will belong to them. This is why we cannot lose heart. Hebrews 10:35-36 says, "Therefore do not cast away your confidence, which has great reward. For you have need of endurance, so that after you have done the will of God, you may receive the promise." We must acknowledge the reality that we are in a war and have confidence in the fact that we will win through the sacrifice made by Jesus.

A declaration of war does two things. The first thing it does is let the enemy know we are coming after them. The second thing a declaration of war does is force a total commitment to win. In his speech on December 8, 1941, Franklin Roosevelt said the following:

> As Commander in Chief of the Army and Navy I have directed that all measures be taken for our defense, that always will our whole nation remember the character of the onslaught against us. No matter how long it may take us to overcome this premeditated invasion, the American people, in their righteous might, will win through to absolute victory. I believe that I interpret the will of the Congress and of the people when I assert that we will not only defend ourselves to the uttermost but will make it very certain that this form of treachery shall never again endanger us. Hostilities exist. There is no blinking at the fact that our people, our territory and our interests are in grave danger. With confidence in our armed forces, with the unbounding determination of our people, we will gain the inevitable triumph. So help us God. I ask that the Congress declare that since the unprovoked and dastardly attack by Japan on Sunday, December 7, 1941, a state of war has existed between the United States and the Japanese Empire.

Roosevelt knew that by making a formal declaration of war against Japan, he could commit all of the United State's resources, if necessary, to defeat that enemy. Until the declaration of war was made, America was not totally committed to defeating Japan. At the time, most Americans were hoping to avoid going to war. However, when Japan attacked Pearl Harbor, they soon realized a response was needed and decided to commit everything America had to defeat her enemy. How many attacks are going to come upon the Christian community before we finally declare war on our enemy? Many lives have been destroyed, yet there is still a lack of total commitment from the Christian community to dedicate *all* they have to defeating the enemy. It is time to respond to the enemy's attacks! It is time to declare war!

War is a very costly and time-consuming ordeal, so there has to be specific reasons for entering a conflict. It would be foolish for a nation to commit its forces without specific objectives. Without these goals, different elements would go different directions, which would result in chaos. In the Gulf War, the United States' objectives were to free Kuwait from Saddam Hussein's tyranny and expel his army from Kuwait in order to remove the threat against Saudi Arabia. Saddam had violated Kuwait's borders, so the allied forces united together to free Kuwait from Iraqi aggression. Once the United States and its allies succeeded in accomplishing that objective, the war ended. Many people faulted our government for stopping the war before Saddam was overthrown. However, that was not one of our objectives for going to war. We needed to stop when we did.

As Christians, we also have a specific objective for going to war with Satan: to get him out of our land so that we can enjoy the abundant life Jesus promised us. We do not need to defeat Satan—he was already defeated when Christ rose from the dead! All we have to do is get him out of our land. That is our sole reason for going to war, and we should not end the war until that objective has been met.

Once the United States defined its objective in the Gulf War, many brilliant military minds went to work to create a plan that would expel the Iraqi army from Kuwait. The plan that was accepted and disseminated to all the troops involved the United States gaining air superiority over the battlefield before it committed any ground forces in the battle. Air superiority is defined as having free access to the airspace above the battle zone while denying the enemy any use of that same airspace. Air superiority is vital in today's combat arenas because it removes one threat axis and allows armies to move swiftly on the ground. When air superiority is gained, the land forces then only have to worry about enemy ground forces. On the other hand, without air superiority, land forces have to move more carefully. If they are caught out in the open, they are sitting ducks for aircraft—specifically aircraft armed with today's technology.

Air superiority alone was not going to win the war. Once the United States' gained air superiority, the Army was employed to remove the enemy out of Kuwait. This battle plan provided victory with very few casualties.

A brilliant mind came up with the spiritual battle plan we are to use in the war we will fight. This battle plan is written down in a book called the Bible. It includes all the tactics and weapons we are to use and gives us the instructions we need to use the authority we have been given. God has ensured the plan has been disseminated to all the troops so that everyone knows what to do. What God now requires is for us to execute His plan. When we do, victory will be ours.

Just as in any war in today's environment, we must maintain air superiority in order to win our spiritual battles. Using angelic power will facilitate superiority over our battlefields. Psalm 103:20-21 says, "Bless the LORD, you His angels, who excel in strength, who do His word, heeding the voice of His word. Bless the LORD, all you His hosts, you ministers of His, who do His pleasure." Speaking God's Word empowers the angels. God's angels are so much more powerful than any of Satan's angels, and when we speak God's Word, His angels give us the spiritual covering we need to enable us to move freely against our enemy. Angels cannot accomplish the objective of removing Satan from our land. Their purpose is to protect (minister to us) while we fight against our enemy.

No one likes war. War is a consuming event that requires all of our resources. However, not going to war will cost us dearly because we are going against an aggressor that has determined to destroy us. God has given us the tools and the spiritual backing to win any war we declare. However, we must be the ones who declare war, because God does not have the authority to do it for us in this world system. When we make a declaration of war against our enemy, we must be ready to go the distance because our enemy is willing to do everything necessary to kill, steal and destroy.

You cannot lose if you use God's battle plan. So *declare war on Satan!* Let him know that you will win because "whatever is born of God overcomes the world" (1 John 5:4). Even if things do not appear to be going the way of victory remember that you are born of God when you accept the sacrifice that Jesus made for you. You are God's child and you have all the rights and privileges a child of the King has. *Do* not lose heart or become discouraged. Be willing to commit everything you have and use the power God has given to you and *go forth and conquer!*

CHAPTER 11

ENTERING THE BATTLE

IT WAS THE night of January 16, 1991, when I found out that our F-16 squadron would start combat missions the next morning. As our squadron gathered to take communion and pray, our commander reminded us that the combat we were about to enter was the one we had trained for since we entered the Air Force. He also reminded us that he would not send us into harm's way if he didn't think we were ready. Even though I had the reassurance of my commander, I still did not get a whole lot of sleep that night. No matter how well you prepare or how good your equipment is, there still is that nagging question, can I do this?

As Christians, we are prepared for battle. As stated earlier, because we live in a hostile environment, we are either in a battle, preparing for a battle, recovering from a battle or helping someone else get through a battle. Like it or not, this is what has been transpiring in our lives ever since we asked Jesus to be Lord of our lives. The trials we have gone through have been our training ground to prepare us for the battles we will face. Our Commander, God Almighty, has declared that we will be prepared when the battle comes. In 1 Corinthians 10:13, He states, "No temptation has overtaken you except such as is common to man; but God is faithful, who will not allow you to be tempted beyond what you are able, but with the temptation will also make the way of escape, that you may be able to bear it." It might seem as though we are not ready for the battles we face, but since we are *in* the situation, we have been declared to be ready by our Commander. We would not be in a battle if we did not have the training or the weapons to win. We must believe that our Commander knows what He is doing.

The night before I was to fly my first combat mission, thousands of thoughts raced through my head. The thoughts that dominated my mind were mostly those of my family, whom I thought I might never see again. As I lay there that night, I realized that if I did not control my emotions, I would not be able to concentrate on the task at hand the next day. It is the same for us Christians. The first thing every Christian must do when entering a battle is control his or her emotions.

Emotions are God-given feelings that every Christian possesses. For a long time, I thought it was wrong for me to express my feelings or have emotions. I got those ideas from a father who had a hard time expressing his feelings. He had been raised in a time when a man was considered weak if he showed any emotions. When I started walking in the fullness of God's Spirit, I found out that emotions were not bad. I can still remember the first time I *really* hugged my dad. It was during the summer between my freshman and sophomore year of college. When I hugged him, he was as stiff as a board, and I am sure he was wondering if he had wasted his money sending me to college. However, my action melted something in him and gave us an ability to physically express our emotions of love toward one another.

Emotions are not bad, but they can cause problems if they are not controlled. The devil knows this fact and will try to get us to a point in which we are listening more to our feelings or emotions than we are to God. If Satan can do that, he has accomplished his objective of moving us from walking in the Spirit to walking in the flesh. If he can successfully get us to that place, he can defeat us.

The way to control our emotions is to meditate on God's Word. Most Christians at one time or another have felt an emotion of fear in the area of their salvation. The only way to counter this fear is to *know* what God says in His Word. Quoting Romans 10:9 and 2 Corinthians 5:17 over and over will give any Christian the confidence he or she needs to realize that he or she is one of God's children—no matter how that person may feel. Every other human emotion must be handled the same way. When emotions begin to move a Christian away from the will of God, he or she must meditate on God's Word in order to get his or her emotions back in line. On my first combat mission, the emotion of fear was very prevalent. However, I realized that I had to do my job no matter what the emotion of fear was telling me. I made a decision to engage the enemy even though I was very afraid. It was a decision that my enemy was hoping I would not make, because my decision to continue caused him great harm.

One emotion that seems to trip up more Christians than any other is anger. Anger is a God-given emotion and is not evil when used in the way God intended. For instance, Jesus was angry when He threw the moneychangers out of the Temple. However, Jesus never let the emotion of anger control Him. Ephesians 4:26 says, "Be angry, and do not sin: do not let the sun go down on your wrath." We cannot be victorious in our spiritual battles as long as we allow anger to rule our lives. Jesus used anger properly when He allowed His anger to motivate Him to aggressively go after sin while loving what God loved. Anger, when not handled properly, will put us in the arena of the flesh and anytime we are in the flesh, Satan can defeat us.

That is why we must control the emotion of anger before we can accomplish anything for God. The way we control anger is the same way we control any other emotion: by meditating on God's Word. When we concentrate on what God says about being angry with others, we are able to handle anger in a proper way. Ephesians 6:12-13 tells us who we are to war against (or get angry with): "For we do not wrestle against flesh and blood, but against principalities, against powers, against the rulers of the darkness of this age, against spiritual hosts of wickedness in the heavenly places." People are not our problem. We are to forgive them their trespasses no matter what they do to us and channel our anger in the direction it belongs—toward our true enemy, which is Satan.

For the Christian, forgiveness is not an option; it is a commandment. Jesus gave the mandate for forgiveness in Luke 17:3-4: "Take heed to yourselves. If your brother sins against you, rebuke him; and if he repents, forgive him. And if he sins against you seven times in a day, and seven times in a day returns to you, saying, 'I repent,' you shall forgive him."

Jesus said that we are to forgive a brother 490 times a day(see Matt. 18:22). But what should we do if he does not repent? Does that give us the right to stay angry and not forgive him? Absolutely not! We are to follow Jesus' example when He forgave the very people who were crucifying Him. They did not ask for His forgiveness, yet He forgave them anyway. Stephen did the same thing when the people were stoning him (see Acts 7). In Matthew 6:14-15, Jesus clarifies this need for us to forgive: "For if you forgive men their trespasses, your heavenly Father will also forgive you. But if you do not forgive men their trespasses, neither will your Father forgive your trespasses."

There have been occasions when I was angry with people and harbored resentment against them. Every time I would go to the Lord, He would constantly remind me of how I had to forgive them. One time

He said, "Before you can deal with the sin in others' lives, you first must deal with the offense in your own life." I argued that I did not want to forgive them because of what they did to me. I was angry, and I wanted to stay that way. But then Jesus would remind me that if I did not forgive these people, God would not forgive me of my sin. God would also remind me that Hebrews 10:30 says, "For we know Him who said, 'Vengeance is Mine, I will repay,' says the Lord. And again, 'The LORD will judge His people.'" Judging people was not my job; it was God's job. My call was to show my love for people by forgiving them and allowing God to handle the issue as He saw fit.

As Christians, we are commanded to "love the Lord your God with all your heart, soul, and mind" (Matt. 22:37). Jesus also said in John 14:23-24, "If anyone loves Me, he will keep My word; and My Father will love him, and We will come to him and make Our home with him. He who does not love Me does not keep My words; and the word which you hear is not Mine but the Father's who sent Me." We are commanded to forgive not based on what has been done to us but based on what God tells us to do. When we do this, power is released through supernatural love. Time and time again as I have walked in what I know is right and forgiven others, I have been given a release that can only come through the Spirit of God. God released a love in me for those people in such a way that I never thought possible.

There are other emotions besides anger that we must control. The reason we have to deal with emotions is because any time emotions are involved, the flesh is also involved. If we enter a battle in an emotional state, we are entering that battle in the flesh. This is why we must control our emotions first and then go fight the battle. Only when we control our emotions will we have the ability to walk in the Spirit and hear the proper orders from our Commander. Without the ability to hear what God is saying, we will always make bad decisions that will get us in trouble or waste time.

One of the biggest mistakes we can make is to suppress our emotions by denying they exist. We must each admit that emotions are involved in the battles we face because suppressing emotions can be as dangerous as not controlling them. All the emotions that we, as humans, possess were given to us by God to help us deal with situations in our lives. Emotions of fear enact the self-preservation mode in us. Emotions of anger can expose things in our lives that need to be dealt with. We must recognize our emotions and then control them if we are going to be victorious in the battles we encounter.

The next step we must take after controlling our emotions is to renew our confidence in the plan God has given us. When I knew that I was going into battle, I reviewed the battle plan over and over. I believed the battle plan would work—even though I did not have proof that it would work—and took confidence in the fact that the people who developed the plan had gone through a previous war. The battles we enter in our Christian lives will not be any different. The Holy Spirit has laid out the plan for victory through the people who gave us the Scriptures. Jesus showed us the plan worked when He walked this earth. Our confidence (or faith) in the plan must be solid if we are to commit to it whole heartily. If we do not have confidence in the plan, we will have a tendency to want to do things our own way, which will always lead to disaster.

After controlling our emotions and putting our confidence in the plan, the next step is to rely on our support. When our squadron went to war during the first Gulf War, there was one thing that we, as pilots, never questioned: the performance of our aircraft. Our maintenance personnel were the best in the business, and we knew the fighters would perform because they had been taken care of by men and women who took their job seriously. When Christians enter a battle, we must know there are people standing behind us who also take their call from God very seriously.

A picture of this kind of support is found in Exodus 17:11-13: "And so it was, when Moses held up his hand, that Israel prevailed; and when he let down his hand, Amalek prevailed. But Moses' hands became heavy; so they took a stone and put it under him, and he sat on it. And Aaron and Hur supported his hands, one on one side, and the other on the other side; and his hands were steady until the going down of the sun. So Joshua defeated Amalek and his people with the edge of the sword." The battles we face as Christians can get very tiring. Satan wants to keep pressure on us in the hopes that we will get tired and quit.

Before Jesus entered the battle of the crucifixion, He spent some time praying in the Garden of Gethsemane. When He went to pray, He asked His disciples to "watch and pray." He was asking for support from His closest friends because He knew how hard the battle was going to be. Unfortunately, the disciples did not understand the situation and went to sleep rather than fight. How many times have we done the same thing for brothers and sisters in Christ who have asked for our help? How many times have people asked us to remember them in prayer only for us to fail to pray for them because we get too busy? If we are not the ones in a battle, we must be willing to use the spiritual gifts that God has given us to support those who are going through battles.

As long as we are in Satan's domain, our lives will be filled with battles. To enter these battles with confidence, we must control our emotions so that we are able to look at the situation objectively and hear from God. We then must review the plan and follow that plan as our Commander has laid it out. In addition, we must rely on our fellow brothers and sisters in Christ to hold up our arms when we get tired. Entering a spiritual battle with these three elements in place will increase the likelihood of victory (the manifestation of a spiritual promise into the natural realm) when the battle is over.

CHAPTER 12

WALKING IN OUR VICTORY

THE BATTLE LINES have been drawn. Satan has decided to wage war against us in some way or another. We did not ask for the battle, but it is here anyway. It could be a sickness, a bill that must be paid, a conflict between people, a persecution or a myriad of other things. Now that we are in this battle, what do we do? Only one thing: *stand!* In Ephesians 6:13-14, Paul puts it this way: "Therefore take up the whole armor of God, that you may be able to withstand in the evil day, and having done all, to stand. Stand therefore, having ..."

In Luke 6:47-49, Jesus talked about the battles we will go through when He spoke of building a house on the rock: "Whoever comes to Me, and hears My sayings and does them, I will show you whom he is like: He is like a man building a house, who dug deep and laid the foundation on the rock. And when the flood arose, the stream beat vehemently against that house, and could not shake it, for it was founded on the rock."

God determined our ability to endure and win the battle before we were put in the position of fighting. First Corinthians 10:13 tells us, "No temptation has overtaken you except such as is common to man; but God is faithful, who will not allow you to be tempted beyond what you are able, but with the temptation will also make the way of escape, that you may be able to bear it." So, if the battle is in the form of a temptation, we can win it! If the battle is in the form of a trial, it is from God and we need to be joyous about it because He has predetermined the outcome. Doubts about whether we can win a battle arise when we begin to look at the circumstances surrounding us instead of looking at Jesus, the author and finisher of our faith (see Heb. 12:2).

Walking out our victory can be the most difficult thing for us to learn because we must learn not to rely on our senses but on God. To consistently walk in victory, we must believe things are happening in a realm we cannot see (the spiritual realm), even if we cannot see anything happening in the realm we can see (the natural realm). To illustrate this, let me relate some events that took place during my first Desert Storm combat mission.

The first day of the Gulf War, my squadron was tasked to be part of a 70-aircraft package that was going against an airfield southwest of Kuwait City. Twenty F-16s from my squadron were the first aircraft to go into the target area, and we were specifically targeted against ten different SAM (Surface-to-Air Missile) sites around the airfield. This type of mission is called a SEAD mission, which means the Suppression of Enemy Air Defenses. As we approached the target area, every aircraft in our flight received warning signals alerting us to the fact that surface-to-air missile radars had locked on to us. When we approached the targeted airfield, we saw missiles being launched and encountered a tremendous amount of anti-aircraft artillery fire.

In the midst of defending myself, I was able to deliver my bombs. As I flew over the target area, I watched my bombs explode a little east of the intended target. My wingman had similar results, and as we began to talk to the other pilots, most of them said that they had the same lack of success. We were very dejected. Our job was to knock out the SAM sites so they could not threaten the fighters coming in to bomb the airfield after us, but the tremendous amount of enemy fire had prevented us from accomplishing our mission.

About two hours after we landed, we received a call from the mission commander (who was at a different airfield) congratulating us on a job well done. He told us that when the fighters came in to bomb the target area, not one missile had been launched against them. We were flabbergasted (although we did not let them know that). We just said, "That is how our squadron does the jobs we are assigned," and left it at that. The only thing we could figure out was the Iraqis shot so many missiles at us that they did not have time to reload before the next wave of fighters came into the target area. After that mission, we no longer called that mission a SEAD mission; we called it a DEAD mission (the Depletion of Enemy Air Defenses).

I told that story to emphasize the fact that even our failures can be victories. We do not know what is happening all around us. When we are going through a battle, at times it will seem that we have messed up.

Remember, God protects our back. What seems like a mess up can turn out to be a victory that we do not recognize. We must trust in the Lord! He will be our strength and support.

We are commanded to stand in the battles we face even though we might not understand the battle completely. However, we can understand certain aspects that are part of every battle, and knowing these elements will increase our ability to stand firm. Look at the events that happened in Matthew 14:25-32:

> Now in the fourth watch of the night Jesus went to them, walking on the sea. And when the disciples saw Him walking on the sea, they were troubled, saying, "It is a ghost!" And they cried out for fear. But immediately Jesus spoke to them, saying, "Be of good cheer! It is I; do not be afraid." And Peter answered Him and said, "Lord, if it is You, command me to come to You on the water." So He said, "Come." And when Peter had come down out of the boat, he walked on the water to go to Jesus. But when he saw that the wind was boisterous, he was afraid; and beginning to sink he cried out, saying, "Lord, save me!" And immediately Jesus stretched out His hand and caught him, and said to him, "O you of little faith, why did you doubt?" And when they got into the boat, the wind ceased.

Now, some might argue that this was not a battle, but it was. Peter had to overcome the natural world with supernatural power. Whenever we have to overcome something in the natural with the supernatural, it is a battle. Remember what Paul says in Galatians 5:17: "For the flesh lusts [or wars] against the Spirit and the Spirit against the flesh." A battle occurs whenever the Spirit has to override anything in this natural world.

This story can help us see the essential elements that are part of every battle. First, notice the predicament in which the disciples found themselves. In Matthew 14:22, Jesus told the disciples to go to the other side of the lake. They had a mandate from their Lord to do something. If Jesus told them they could go to the other side, it meant they were empowered to do so. However, when the winds and waves started crashing around them and they saw Jesus walking on the water, they were afraid.

Fear is one of the essential elements of every battle we encounter. Our natural mind has a mechanism of survival that activates fear whenever it does not understand what is going on around it. Although this can be good—it can alert us to a dangerous situation and compel us to take action—it can also interfere with what God has told us to do. Natural fear is part of the world system, of which Satan is the head. Satan's nature is to bring on the emotion of fear within us.

In the story in Matthew, fear was now getting in the way of what Jesus had told the disciples to do: go to the other side of the lake. Peter was the only disciple who recognized what needed to happen next. Once he heard Jesus' voice, he controlled his fear by refocusing on whom Jesus was and what He said to do.

God's Word is the second element that will be part of any battle. When the natural world system (filled with fear) and the Word of God come face to face, all the necessary elements are present for a battle. When Peter found himself in this spiritual battle, he had to choose between what his natural mind could understand and what Jesus was telling him to do. The moment Peter chose to climb out of the boat and walk on the water, he allowed Jesus' words to take priority over his natural understanding. Peter made a decision based on Jesus' words rather than on his natural understanding of how things worked.

In a previous chapter, I told the story of how my children had a hard time jumping into the deep end of the swimming pool when they were little. I was determined not to allow fear to rule their lives, so I would get into the water and assure them that I would catch them and not let them sink. It amused me to watch them look at the water and then at me. I kept assuring them, but they would continue to look at the water and then look at me. They knew how much I loved them and believed in my protection capabilities, but they still had a hard time making the decision to jump in. Once they allowed their confidence in me to overcome their fear of the water, they would finally jump into the pool.

When battles happen, we must choose whether we will believe what our natural senses (which are controlled by our emotions) are telling us or believe in what God is telling us in His Word. This is the essence of every battle we encounter. When we recognize that every conflict boils down to those two factors, it will be easier for us to understand what we must do to win in every situation.

Just as my children had to have confidence in me to overcome their fear, we must have unwavering confidence in our Father so that we can overcome our fears. First John 5:4-5 says, "For whatever is born of God overcomes the world. And this is the victory that has overcome the world—our faith. Who is he who overcomes the world, but he who believes that Jesus is the Son of God?" As I mentioned, if we have been born again, we have the ability to overcome anything in this natural world. But knowledge of this fact alone will not make us victorious. Only faith in the One who backs up that statement will enable us to walk in victory. That is why Jesus told us in Matthew 6:33 to "seek first the kingdom of God and His righteousness." We must first look to our source before we will see our victory.

As I flew into the battle zone during my first combat sortie, I had to evade all the threats that were coming against me. However, there was a point when I had to forget about the threats and concentrate on the mission goals. I can still remember saying to myself, *If I continue these evasive maneuvers, I'll go past the point of being able to deliver my bombs on target.* It was at this point that I determined to ignore the threats and deliver my bombs against the intended target. In the same way, when we are in our battles, our victory will come when we forget about the threats coming against us, disregard the fear and focus on our mission goal: to deliver a devastating blow to our enemy.

Before we get to that point, we will encounter all sorts of things that will try to distract us and defeat us. In the story of Peter walking on the water, he faced the distractions of the winds and the waves. If we are facing sickness, it could be a bad report from the doctor. If we need a financial miracle, it could be another bill that shows up in the mail. If we allow these distractions to overtake us, as Peter did, we will fail to achieve the victory God desires for us.

The way to victory is through faith. When Peter failed, Jesus said to him, "O you of little faith, why did you doubt?" (Matt. 14:31). Jesus was telling Peter (and us) that the victory was there for him if he only believed in His words. Our victory will come the same way—through faith in the Word that God speaks to us.

As I stated previously, one of the main aspects of faith is the fact that it is unseen. Our battles are fought in the spiritual realm. If we can figure out how something will work out, it is not faith. True faith means believing something will happen because God said it would and because we trust Him to do what He says. That assurance cannot come from a casual understanding of God's Word. It comes only from meditating on His Word.

When God speaks the spoken word to our spirits, faith is increased in our lives. That is why meditating on God's Word is vital when we are in a battle. Psalm 1:2 says, "And in His law he meditates day and night." Joshua 1:8 says, "This Book of the Law shall not depart from your mouth, but you *shall meditate in it day and night,* that you may observe to do according to *all* that is written in it" (emphasis added).

There is one more aspect about this story in Matthew that we need to examine before we move on. Peter did not win this battle. He failed to adhere to Jesus' words and trusted in what his senses were telling him instead of in Jesus. As a result, he began to sink. "But when he saw [physical senses] that the wind was boisterous, he was afraid [yielded to the emotion of fear], and beginning to sink he cried out, saying, 'Lord save me!' And immediately Jesus stretched out His hand and caught him, and said to him, 'O you of little faith, why did you doubt?'" (Matt. 14:30-31). Jesus was there to rescue Peter when he failed. We cannot neglect the fact that there will be casualties of war. We also need to be prepared to rescue people when they fail.

The Air Force commits a tremendous amount of resources to rescue downed aircrew. These missions are called Sandy Missions, and their sole purpose is to rescue those who are shot down while executing their part of the battle plan. If an airman is shot down, there are times when entire packages of aircraft are diverted to help rescue the downed airman. Too bad we do not have that same mentality in the Christian world! All too often, good Christian people are abandoned in the battle zone. When Peter failed, Jesus rescued him. We need to do the same for our brothers and sisters in Christ.

Our goal is to win every battle we encounter. To achieve this goal, we must make a decision to keep fighting no matter what our senses are telling us. In the next chapter, I want to relay some of the things that must be done when the battle seems to be going nowhere.

CHAPTER 13

KEEPING OUR VICTORIES

WHEN BATTLES COME, whether big or small, the way to victory remains the same and the methodology of the world system, which we are fighting, is the same. The Spirit will give us inputs that we can win, while the natural realm will try to instill fear within us. These inputs from our spirit and the natural world system will begin to go at each other in our minds. Our "soul part" (our mind, will and emotions) must now choose which set of inputs it will follow. The number one hindrance to victory is failure of our minds to choose God's option of standing.

The soul part of humans was created by God to be our "chooser." It was created to choose paths that will protect the part of us that houses our spirit. In this earth system, the flesh houses the Spirit. First Corinthians 3:16-17 says, "Do you not know that you are the temple of God and that the Spirit of God dwells in you? If anyone defiles the temple of God, God will destroy him. For the temple of God is holy, which temple you are." So, while we still have a body made of flesh, our soul (mind, will, and emotions) will naturally make decisions to protect the flesh based on what it knows.

Until we are in communication with God through the Spirit, our soul only gets fleshly inputs and, therefore, only makes fleshly (or carnal) decisions. In the first part of Romans 8, Paul discusses how once we come into contact with the spiritual, God has access to change our minds based on the gospel of Christ. In my own life, I did not make a decision to follow Jesus until I realized it was in my best interest, eternally, to do so. Once my soul heard the words of salvation, it understood that to live eternally was the best thing to protect the spirit, so I made a decision (an act of my will) to accept Jesus' sacrifice for my sins and be saved.

When we are in a battle, the soul will follow the course of action that it believes will preserve the flesh and preserve a housing place for our spirit part. Romans 6:17 tells us that before we were saved, we were slaves to sin. The reason we were slaves to sin is that only one source of information (ungodly information) was getting to our soul, and therefore it could only choose the ways of the flesh. However, once our spirit was reborn and could communicate with God, two sources of information became available: the Spirit and the flesh. The problem for most Christians is that they allow too many inputs from the natural world to come into their minds. Solely based on the amount of time they spend in each system, most Christians will have more inputs from the world system (TV, movies, music, books, magazines, ungodly friends) than inputs from the Spirit (God's Word, anointed teachers, godly friends).

There was a great man of God who went to be with Jesus several years ago. When people came to him for prayer, he would ask them what scriptures they were standing on for their victory. The reply he most often heard was, "Nothing in particular." When he heard this, he would reply, "Then that is what you will get: Nothing in particular." When we ignore God's Word, we prevent Him from speaking to our spirits and do not give our souls anything to stand on from the spiritual side. When our souls do not have anything to stand on, they will revert to their natural function, which is self-preservation. The result is fear, and fear will result in failure.

Once we make a decision to stand, we also have to make a corresponding effort to get into God's Word. We have to get the world system out and get God's system in. In our family, when there is a sickness in our home, the rule is that there is no television, games or anything of the world system until that sickness is removed. This allows us to focus all of our efforts on hearing God's Word in order to give our souls something to stand on. As we begin to choose God's Word over the inputs from the world, the sickness bows its knee to the Word and the results we were praying for begin to be manifested.

Once we have made a decision to stand and declare to this world system, "Fight's on" (a term used by fighter pilots when they train against each other), we must continually assess how the battle is going. One time, my second son was very sick. He had a high temperature and was miserable. My wife and I began to read and meditate on God's Word. We quoted the Bible, sang praises to God, and did all the things we knew to bring His healing power to my son. However, my son did not get better. In times of war, there will always be tactics that do not seem to work. We knew it had been predetermined that my son was healed (because God had said he was in His Word), but we were not seeing the manifestation of the healing. When we reached the point we were not getting the results promised by God, we began to ask God if we were doing anything outside of His Word or if we were to continue to stand on the belief that my son was healed.

If there is a promise in the Word that does not manifest itself in the natural, the first place to look for reasons is not with God but with us. My wife and I sat down and began to evaluate our lives. As we talked, God revealed to us that a minor division had arisen between us. We forgave each other, and as soon as we did, my son's fever instantly left him. As long as there was any strife and division, God's Spirit could not operate as He desired. As we went through the battle, we changed our attack according to what God showed us. Our victory was assured, but my wife and I had to fix some things in our relationship before God's Spirit could work on our behalf.

I mentioned earlier that one of the superior traits of the American soldier is his or her ability to improvise and change tactics when something is not working. We must do the same thing when we are in a battle. We cannot just read and meditate on God's Word and expect victory; we must also analyze how things are going and be ready to change anything in our lives that God reveals. Our Commander will show us if there are areas of disobedience, if we are not walking in love, if we have strife or division in our lives, or if we have misidentified the source of the battle.

Disobedience is a major hindrance to winning battles. To illustrate this, look at the story of Joshua and the children of Israel in Joshua 7. Joshua had just defeated Jericho. In Joshua 6:18, God had said to Joshua, "And you, by all means abstain from the accursed things, lest you become accursed when you take of the accursed things, and make the camp of Israel a curse, and trouble it." In chapter seven, we see that a man named Achan had taken some accursed things and hidden them in his tent. As a result of this disobedience, the children of Israel lost the battle of Ai. When the people of Israel asked the reason, God responded, "Israel has sinned, and they have also transgressed My covenant which I commanded them. For they have even taken some of the accursed things, and have both stolen and deceived; and they have also put it among their own stuff. Therefore the children of Israel could not stand before their enemies, but turned their backs before their enemies, because they have become doomed to destruction. Neither will I be with you anymore, unless you destroy the accursed from among you" (Josh. 7:11-13). God had already determined the victory that He wanted for the children of Israel, but disobedience to His word prevented them from walking in their victory.

Our battles will be the same. When we do not receive what we have been promised in God's Word, the first place we should look is to our own lives to see if we have been disobedient in one way or another. I remember one time we were having financial struggles. I could not figure out why we were falling farther and farther behind when God's Word promises that He will provide all of our needs (see Phil. 4:19). When I inquired of the Lord, He told me I had been disobedient by giving some money away that He had not instructed me to give.

We were supporting a couple who were going through Bible School. Before we gave anything, my wife and I had prayed and received a certain amount that we were to give. We asked the couple if they wanted it all at one time or in installments, and they said a monthly amount would be better for them. We began to send them a monthly check, but when we reached the amount God told us to give, there were still two months left in the school year. Feeling bad about cutting off support with a couple of months remaining, I decided to continue sending them the same amount for the next two months. Even though I was doing something nice, I was being disobedient to what God had told me to do. As a result, He could not help me win my battles in the financial realm because I was not listening to Him. I repented and, just as Jesus rescued Peter, God rescued me and made our finances whole.

Disobedience can be a very subtle problem. We can be so easily deceived into thinking that we are doing something good when we really are disobeying what God says. Do not give up the excellence of the blessings of God for something that is good. Read God's Word, because it will judge the intent of your heart to see if you are walking in what God wants or in what you want (see Heb. 4:12).

There is one form of disobedience that will disallow victories in your life quicker than anything else. Jesus said in Matthew 22:37-40, "You shall love the LORD your God with all your heart, with all your soul, and with all your mind. This is the first and great commandment. And the second is like it: 'You shall love your neighbor as yourself.'" The fastest way a Christian will be defeated is if he or she does not walk in love. Love is the essential element of who God is. First John 4:8 tells us, "God is love." Galatians 5:6 says that "faith works through love." So, although we must have faith to win our battles, we must also walk in love. To know love, we must know God, for God is love. When we do not walk in love, we cannot walk in faith. If we do not walk in faith, we cannot walk in victory.

If battles are not going the way the Word says they should, we should next examine whether there is strife or division in our relationships. James 3:13-16 says, "Who is wise and understanding among you? Let him show by good conduct that his works are done in the meekness of wisdom. But if you have bitter envy and self-seeking in your hearts, do not boast and lie against the truth. This wisdom does not descend from above, but is earthly, sensual, demonic. For where envy and self-seeking exist, confusion and every evil thing are there." Satan is the master of deception. He knows that if he can get us to look after our own interests, we will fall into envy and strife. If he can get us into that position, we are doomed to failure.

If we are not walking in faith, we cannot please God (see Heb. 11:6), and victory will escape us. It is important to note in the above passage in James that "every evil thing" is encompassed in envy and self-seeking. That is why it is so important to make sure that we are walking in love and are not just trying to get what we want. We cannot allow ourselves to be defeated so easily. We must submit to the commandment of love and throw off envy and self-seeking.

Finally, to keep our victory, we need to be sure that we have identified the battle correctly. When I went through the Air Force's Fighter Weapon School, I was taught how to properly analyze a combat scenario so that I could make a proper decision on how to employ the aircraft's weapons. As Christians, we must also be able to correctly assess what is going on so that we can properly identify the threat and employ the right spiritual weapons. Too many times, Christians do not know how or why they are in certain battles. Wisdom from God will assist in this area. Communication with the Father will tell us how to deal with the true issues instead of just warring against the symptoms. Just handling symptoms will distract us. Until we get to the heart of an issue, it will be very difficult for us to win a battle.

There will be times when we will do everything in line with God's Word and yet not see His promises manifested in our lives. What do we do then? Go back to step one: make a decision to stand. That decision does not have a timeline with it. It is a decision to stand until God's will is done on earth as it is done in heaven. Faith is realizing that we have what we believe right now. However, the manifestation of what we have now, in the spiritual realm, can take some time to manifest in the natural realm.

Do not quit! Wait for the promise to come to pass! Do not allow negative confessions to enter in just because you cannot see the manifestation of God's promise. Be patient and believe that the promise is coming. David said in Psalm 40:1-3, "I waited patiently for the LORD; and He inclined to me, and heard my cry. He also brought me up out of a horrible pit, out of the miry clay, and set my feet upon a rock, and established my steps. He has put a new song in my mouth—Praise to our God; many will see it and fear, and will trust in the LORD." The writer of Hebrews tells us how Abraham received what God promised him: "And so, after he had patiently endured, he obtained the promise" (6:15). James 5:7-8 says, "Therefore be patient, brethren, until the coming of the Lord. See how the farmer waits for the precious fruit of the earth, waiting patiently for it until it receives the early and latter rain. You also be patient. Establish your hearts, for the coming of the Lord is at hand." Patience is a fruit of the Spirit. It is a confident declaration that we will stand no matter what! When the devil sees our resolve, he will realize that he can't win and flee the battle.

One thing I like to do when things seem as if they are taking a long time to manifest is go on the offensive. If God has told me that I'm doing everything He has asked of me and I still do not see the manifestation of victory, I start going after Satan's realm. If he is going to slap me, I have determined that I will slap him back. I look for more opportunities to witness, I give more of my time and my money and I look for parts of Satan's kingdom I can go after. Likewise, if you are in a time of waiting, start a witnessing campaign in your neighborhood and shout out the manifold wisdom of God to the principalities and powers (see Eph. 3:10). Most of the time when I do this, I see a shift from waiting for the manifestation to realizing victory, because Satan cannot stand being beat on. He is a coward by nature, and when cowards are confronted, they flee.

Walking in victory should be the normal existence for a Christian. Jesus Christ has given us complete authority in this world system (see Matt. 28:18). We have spiritual weapons that are mighty for pulling down strongholds (see 2 Cor. 10:4). We have people that have walked in faith before us (see Heb. 12:1). However, we also have an enemy that is crafty. We must be diligent to follow God's commands in order to consistently walk in victory. God's will is for us to have an abundant life. To do that, we have to adhere to His ways of doing things. His ways of doing things have nothing to do with this world system, and therefore they will always conflict with our minds. But if we will trust God and believe in His words, we will walk in this world system as Jesus walked. We will accomplish greater things (in number) than Jesus did while He was here (see John 14:12). We will defeat our enemies at every turn—they will come at us one way and have to flee from us in seven ways (see Deut. 28:7). There will not be one form of evil that can get to us or even come near our dwelling (see Ps. 91:10).

As we walk in our victories, others will begin to notice and see the greatness of our God. Our victories will lead to opportunities to share how good God is. We will have opportunities to express our love for Him and will rescue many that are lost and dying in this world system. The fight will not be easy, but it will be worth it.

Paul expressed the end of his life this way in 2 Timothy 4:7-8: "I have fought the good fight, I have finished the race, I have kept the faith. Finally, there is laid up for me the crown of righteousness, which the Lord, the righteous Judge, will give to me on that Day, and not to me only but also to all who have loved His appearing." If we are saved, we, like Paul, will ultimately win. However, we should never be satisfied with ultimate victory. We should be people who take the fight to our enemy and storm the gates of hell. We should not let our enemy have one prisoner too many. Our family members, friends and neighbors deserve more out of us. Let us be an army that pleases God—an army of sons and daughters who walk in love, power and victory, just as the first-born Son showed us how it should be done and be consistent winners in this life!

May God be praised! Amen!

Pleasant Word

To order additional copies of this title call:
1-877-421-READ (7323)
or please visit our Web site at
www.pleasantwordbooks.com

If you enjoyed this quality custom-published book,
drop by our Web site for more books and information.

www.winepressgroup.com

"Your partner in custom publishing."

LaVergne, TN USA
13 February 2011
216317LV00004B/273/P